THE GODS OF BUSINESS

The Intersection of Faith and the Marketplace

TODD ALBERTSON

Published by:

Trinity Alumni Press
Los Angeles, California, USA
www.trinityalumni.org

First Edition, March 2007

Library of Congress Control Number: 2007900080

ISBN: 978-0-6151-3800-8

Printed in the United States of America

This book is dedicated to my father Clarence who taught me that there are ethics in business. He did this without piety or proclamation, but rather by how he acted on a daily basis.

ACKNOWLEDGEMENT

I should like to start with special acknowledgement for the encouragement and support given by my best friend T.J. She patiently put up with the time I spent with writing activities and kept me excited about this project when I wanted to give up.

This book would not have been possible without countless numbers of "guinea pigs." For at least three years they heard me lecture about the subjects covered in these pages. I can only imagine what the first group went through and probably should apologize to them, but their patient attention and polite questions, combined with that of subsequent groups, gave me the great gift of refining my thoughts.

All thoughts need tempering, and for the fire and cold water of that process I must thank my doctoral advisor, Professor A. Norashkharian. His thoughts helped hammer a concept into to a completed work.

I have a very special thank you to my editor, Jeff Andrus. He is an award-winning screenwriter, a wise and patient counselor, and a good friend.

Because this was my first book, I genuinely appreciate the knowledgeable help provided by the Trinity Alumni Press staff, especially that of Pat Morgan.

Some of the material in this book was inspired by conversations, emails, thoughts and suggestions from a variety of students and colleagues, most of whom remain nameless but not unappreciated in my heart.

CONTENTS

PART ONE

◉

FOREWORD

PART TWO

◉

RELIGIONS ORIGINATING IN
CHINA AND JAPAN

PART THREE

☉

RELIGIONS ORIGINATING IN INDIA

PART FOUR

⊙

RELIGIONS ORIGINATING IN THE MIDDLE EAST

PART FIVE

⊙

RELIGIONS ORIGINATING IN
SECULAR POSTMODERNISM

PART SIX

⊙

EPILOGUE

PART ONE

◉

FOREWORD

A WORD TO THE READER

This book was a long time in the making. Its genesis can be traced to the late 1990's when a business I owned had strategic relationships with two companies that were very religious in their organizational cultures. The principals of each company prayed before meals, shut down operations for observance of religious holidays and openly discussed the importance of faith in daily life.

Their religions clearly promoted ethics that taught lying, cheating and dishonesty were wrong. I assumed that these standards would be put into action in everyday business practices. I was mistaken! When the microscopic veneer of faith was pulled away, I found far more dishonesty and unethical behavior than any I had dealt with in the past or would in the future. It was as if the executives had never embraced a moral code of conduct. I faced a conundrum.

I didn't have to be an anthropologist or a sociologist to know that people sincerely hold religious convictions. But I didn't have to spend much time watching the nightly news to see that religious faith didn't always translate well into individual or corporate conduct. I explored this idea in my doctoral thesis entitled *The Impact of Religious Worldview on Business Ethics and Practices in Twentieth Century Western Society.* That thesis gave rise to this book.

Writing this book was an exhausting experience. The first draft was well over 1,500 pages with footnotes that were longer than the final published version. The subjects of worldview, religion and ethics are so wide-sweeping that I could have kept writing and writing and writing, only to produce a document so detailed in its analysis as to be completely unusable except as a doorstop. The businessperson in me decided there was not much of a market for doorstops. Therefore I rewrote and edited for a clean, clear practical guide—a jargon-free explanation of the world's major religions and how those faiths intersect with business.

With exception of the first and last chapters, every other chapter covers a major religion and is broken into the following sections:

1. Introduction

2. History

3. Sacred Texts

4. Selected Readings

5. Core Beliefs

6. Branches

7. In The Marketplace

Sacred Texts offers a convenient summary of important writings. In order to aid appreciation of the tone and style of sacred texts, Selected Readings then follow. The excerpts come from public domain English translations and merely highlight the vast treasuries of religious writings. Formatting is purposely kept as close to the original documents as possible. This makes the reading visually similar to what the authors originally intended.

This book will frustrate some because I don't spoon-feed the reader, as if you were unable to draw a conclusion for yourself. The sections applying religion to the marketplace are short compared to preceding sections. My reasoning is: once understanding is gained from a religion's history, core beliefs and sacred texts, the market application is often straightforward and self-explanatory.

I do not decide the issues of the present day. I do try to lay out the bare bones of belief of the major religions, the basic ideas and values that many religions share towards business, and the most likely ways that people express their various faiths.

I hope I have kept *The Gods of Business* simple but subtle, letting you the reader draw your own conclusions.

Todd Albertson

CHAPTER 1

THE DILEMMA

I see in the near future a crisis approaching that unnerves me and causes me to tremble for the safety of my country.... Corporations have been enthroned and an era of corruption in high places will follow, and the money of the country will endeavour to prolong its reign by working upon the prejudices of the people until all wealth is aggregated in a few hands and the Republic is destroyed.

I feel at this moment more anxiety for the safety of my country than ever before, even in the midst of war.

President Abraham Lincoln

PRINCE HENRY THE NAVIGATOR

Prince Henry the Navigator (1394–1460 C.E.) was the son of King João of Portugal. Henry organized and financed many sea expeditions. His most famous were in search of a sea route to the rich spice trade of the Indies and along the way to explore the west coast of Africa.

Prince Henry encountered much difficulty in persuading his captains to sail beyond Cape Bojador in the southern Sahara. They believed the legend that only the "Green Sea of Darkness" existed beyond this point. They thought the sun was so close to the Earth that a person's skin would turn black. The sea boiled. Ships would catch on fire. Hidden monsters lurked, waiting to smash the ships and eat their crews!

On the first attempt Henry sent his ships with orders to keep close to the coastline. A couple of weeks after they left, they returned to Portugal. Their captains told the prince they could not find a sea route to India because they had come to the "end of the world." Henry sent out thirteen more ships, and each one came back with the same story. From our armchair in history it is easy to see how askew that worldview was. It depended on prejudices that few thought about or were willing to change in the face of evidence.

The English word "worldview" comes from the German word *weltanschauung*, which means a "look onto the world." The term originally was used to refer to a common concept of reality shared by a particular group of people who were generally bound by culture or ethnicity. The word has been expanded over time to reflect how an individual views the world and interacts within it.

On the fourteenth voyage commissioned by Prince Henry, the ship was blown off course, and the crew could no longer see the African coastline. The captain pointed his ship's bow east and a few days later came upon Africa again, surprised that his ship had somehow bypassed the Green Sea of Darkness.

But a few years later the captain re-discovered his worst fear. He had announced a sea route to India. Now as he sailed south along the Spanish Sahara, he came to a major rock shoal. On the approach the water became shallower and shallower. Strange currents began to develop.

The captain and crew were positive that the end of the world they had missed earlier was now about to destroy them.

Undoubtedly that is how they felt. The limits of their ability to discover had nothing to do with their bravery or their goodness, nor was it charted on any accurate map of the world. Rather, the limits were mapped unconsciously by what they had subjectively envisioned—their worldview.

Why is worldview important in business? Because people of faith will approach all of their endeavors with grains of objective truth. Whatever those grains may be, they are going to be washed, sieved and filtered through subjective and unconscious ways of comprehending, acting and explaining. Some grains will be overlooked, forgotten or thrown away as inconvenient. Hence, like the Portuguese sailors of Prince Henry's day, the modern businessperson's religious worldview provides a mental map of how to conduct business.

RELIGION

The adage, "Never discuss sex, politics or religion," makes for a very dull evening. Arguments about them, however, can excite the evening to the point of breaking up the party and destroying friendships. Perhaps the problem is the cumulative effect of passions. If so, dropping the first two subjects might allow for a more peaceful discussion of the third. Alas, religion has a lot to say about sex and politics. Consequently this book is bound to ignite passions. My hope is that it also inspires thought.

A simple definition of religion is a belief in a supernatural or spiritual being(s), and the practices and ethical code that result from that belief. Beliefs give religion its mind; rituals give religion its form; and ethics give religion its heart.

Each religion teaches its unique truths about the world, humanity and humanity's relationship to the supernatural. A religion also details how its followers achieve enlightenment (what some would call holiness; and others, peace of mind), and why its beliefs are important steps in this journey. Through these belief systems, religions teach about misconduct or sin, suffering and hope, life and death, and whatever comes after.

Judging the prominence of the world's religions raises all kinds of problems because the criteria are so subjective. Adherents.com skips the problems by listing the top world religions in terms of sheer numbers. According to Adherents' count of participants, the top fifteen religions of the world are:

Rank	Religion	Adherents
1	Christianity	2.1 billion
2	Islam	1.3 billion
3	Secular/Nonreligious/Agnostic/Atheist	1.1 billion
4	Hinduism	900 million
5	Chinese traditional religion	394 million
6	Buddhism	376 million
7	Primal/Indigenous	300 million
8	African Traditional & Diasporic	100 million
9	Sikhism	23 million
10	Juche	19 million
11	Spiritism	15 million
12	Judaism	14 million
13	Baha'i	7 million
14	Jainism	4.2 million
15	Shintoism	4 million

In this book we will look at nine of these religions. Alphabetically they are: Buddhism, Christianity, Confucianism, Hinduism, Islam, Judaism, Secular Postmodernism, Shintoism and Sikhism.

Adherents' third ranked religion—Secular/Nonreligious/Agnostic/Atheist—is a mouthful. That is why in this book the category is called Secular Postmodernism.

Rather than deal with the entirety of the fifth ranked religion, the focus has been narrowed on the major component of Chinese traditional religion, i.e., Confucianism.

Judaism, ranked twelfth, and Shintoism, the fifteenth largest, have been included for discussion in this book.

Excluded are Primal/Indigenous, African Traditional & Diasporic, Juche, Spiritism, Baha'i and Jainism. In my opinion their practitioners and worldviews are not major forces in the global marketplace (at least in comparison to other religions).

BUSINESS ETHICS

The ethics of a religion are both personal and corporate. Some ethics show followers how to live their own lives while others set standards of conduct for entire societies.

Ethics dictate the way people should live with one another and with nature. By following a religion's ethical code, practitioners believe they can live good, decent, compassionate, just and loving lives. Ethics give religion its moral force and universal message.

Business ethics are the rules and principles within the context of commerce. Because different worldviews have different business ethics, contrasts frequently emerge during business transactions. A more detailed discussion about the differences will follow in subsequent chapters.

Business ethics can be self-serving and affect a company's overall mission. For example, if a company's main purpose is to merely maximize short-term profits for its stockholders, members of the governing board might think it unethical to favor the rights of employees, customers, society and the community.

Business ethics play out most frequently in issues concerning relations with different companies that are suppliers, buyers or competitors, as well as with government regulators. Political contributions and lobbying efforts influence the latter. Bribery may be included. Just as advertising is meant to sell product, public relations are meant to sell the company's image to the wider world. Coloring the truth may be part of PR, sometimes to the point of outright lying. The ethics of these endeavors almost always reveal underlying theories about property rights versus environmental impact, individualism verses collectivism, the role of self-interest versus the needs of society or future generations. In some cases the company may be fighting the good fight against centralized government tyranny or local mob rule.

REFERENCES AND FURTHER READING

Cavanagh, Gerald F., and Arthur F. McGovern. *Ethical Dilemmas in the Modern Corporation.* Upper Saddle River: Prentice Hall, 1988.

Hartman, Laura P. *Perspectives in Business Ethics.* Columbus: McGraw-Hill/Irwin, 2004.

Liebig, James E. *Business Ethics: Profiles in Civic Virtue.* Golden: Fulcrum Publishing, 1991.

Stackhouse, Max. *On Moral Business: Classical and Contemporary Resources for Ethics in Economic Life.* Grand Rapids: Wm. B. Eerdmans Publishing Company, 1995.

Rothman, Howard, and Mary Scott. *Companies with a Conscience: Intimate Portraits of Twelve Firms That Make a Difference, Third Edition.* Indianapolis: The Publishing Cooperative/Myers Templeton Books, 2003.

Seglin, Jeffrey L. *The Good, the Bad, and Your Business: Choosing Right When Ethical Dilemmas Pull You Apart.* New York: John Wiley & Sons, Inc., 2000.

Solomon, Robert C. *Above the Bottom Line: An Introduction to Business Ethics.* Orlando: Harcourt, 1993.

PART TWO

◉

RELIGIONS ORIGINATING IN CHINA AND JAPAN

CHAPTER 2

CONFUCIANISM

Fellow-feeling . . .

Do not do unto others

what thou wouldst not

they should do unto thee.

Analects 15:23

Confucianism is the world's fifth largest religion with some 394 million practitioners worldwide. Confucianism literally means The School of the Scholars or less precisely "The Religion of Confucius." It is widely debated whether Confucianism is a religion or an ethical and philosophical system based on the teachings of Kung Fu-Tzu (Confucius), a Chinese philosopher who lived between 551–479 B.C.E.

Some do not believe Confucianism to be a religion because it lacks formal worship or a meditation component. Yet it has a strong religious-like focus on ritual and a distinctive worldview that dictates its practitioners' outlook on life. Regardless of whether Confucianism is a religion, a philosophy or a melding of both along with other influences, Confucius' beliefs became the standard in Chinese politics and scholarship. They were eventually recognized as the official Chinese Imperial belief system. That system has had immense impact on Chinese and other East Asian societies, including religious movements that have arisen in other cultures.

Perhaps the best-known distinction between Confucianism and other religions is the lack of a central, authoritative God figure. Confucius receives ritual respect from followers but is not worshipped as God.

HISTORY

Confucius spent a great deal of his adulthood working in administrative positions within the government. As an intellectual he worried about the troubled times in which he lived, and traveled widely to spread his political ideas and to influence many of the warlords contending for supremacy in China.

Confucius believed in the perfectibility of humanity by the cultivation of the mind. He stressed the importance of pursuing peace and equity, devotion to parents and to rituals, learning, self-control and socially just activity. His teachings moved from being philosophical to religious when people began acting in a "correct" way, following proper protocol and engaging in ceremonial etiquette.

Confucius introduced the idea of meritocracy, which led to the introduction of the Imperial examination system in China in 165 B.C.E. As this system evolved over the following centuries, anyone who wished to become a government official had to prove his worth by passing written examinations. A revolutionary concept at the time, meritocracy became the foundation for modern civil services throughout the world.

Confucius' establishment of Rujia, the School of the Literati, produced public officials with a strong sense of national pride and duty. Confucius said that praiseworthy were those kings who left their kingdoms to those most qualified to manage them, rather than to their elder sons as tradition dictated. The ethics underlying Confucian thought are revealed in the Hundred Schools of Thought, developed by his disciples and their descendants.

Debated during the Warring States Period and outlawed during the Qin Dynasty, Confucianism survived its suppression partly due to the discovery of a trove of Confucian classics hidden in the walls of a scholar's house.

Confucianism was chosen by Han Wudi as a political system to govern the Chinese Imperial state. Despite its loss of influence during the Tang Dynasty, Confucian doctrine remained an anchor of Chinese thought for 2,000 years until it was attacked during the Cultural Revolution in the People's Republic of China in 1966 C.E. Although it was outlawed, Confucianism never left the hearts of the Chinese people and has had a contemporary renaissance in Mainland China.

Besides the culture of China, the societies most strongly influenced by Confucianism include Japan, Korea, Singapore, Taiwan, Vietnam, and the territories of Hong Kong and Macau.

SACRED TEXTS

The Five Classics (Wu Ching) and *The Four Books (Ssu Shu)* are 2,000-year-old books that detail Confucian ideas on law, society, government, education, literature and religion. Although not strictly holy texts, these works became the core curriculum in Chinese universities and are still studied today.

The Five Classics

(1) *The Book of History* was written during the Han dynasty (206 B.C.E. –220 C.E.) and describes events dating back to the Third Millennium B.C.E. This book contains the sayings and rules of wise and wicked rulers of past dynasties. It also details why heaven supported the wise rulers and opposed the wicked ones.

(2) *The Book of Songs/Poetry* contains over 300 songs and poems as old as 1000–500 B.C.E.

(3) *The Book of Rites* details Chinese religious practices from the 8th to the 5th Centuries B.C.E.

(4) *The Book of Changes* contains 64 symbolic hexagrams that, if interpreted correctly, followers of Confucius believe offer insight into human behavior. This book dates back to around 3000 B.C.E. and is considered one of the most popular holy books among Eastern religions.

(5) *The Book of Spring and Autumn* is a chronology of Confucius' home state of Lu. He may have dictated the book which was compiled sometime between 722-481 B.C.E.

The Four Books

These books served as the basis of Chinese civil service and government until the early 20th Century. They were originally published separately until they were compiled as a single volume in 1190 C.E.

(1) *The Great Learning* is a book of instructions on the correct way to perform rituals. Written between 500-200 B.C.E., its primary theme is the effect of a ruler's integrity on government.

(2) *Doctrine of the Mean* emphasizes "the Way" toward self-realization or the perfectly cultivated self, and is the most mystical of Confucian writings.

(3) *The Analects* are sayings of Confucius compiled by his disciples more than 70 years after his death in 479 B.C.E. The collection con-

tains the majority of *The Four Books* and details the basic tenants of Confucian thought, such as perpetuation of culture, respectful conduct of affairs, loyalties to superiors and keeping promises. It includes vignettes of Confucius' own life.

(4) *The Book of Mencius* interprets Confucian thought through the teachings of Mencius, one of the most esteemed Confucian scholars. Mencius asserted that righteousness is more important than life itself. He believed that individuals could achieve the Way only though constant self-refinement.

Unlike most Western philosophers, Confucius did not rely on deductive reasoning to convince his listeners. Instead, he used dictum and aphorism in a highly contextualized manner that often frustrates Western readers who are not familiar with Eastern circular thought.

SELECTED READINGS

BOOK I *HSIO R*

CHAP. I. The Master said, "Is it not pleasant to learn with a constant perseverance and application?

Is it not delightful to have friends coming from distant quarters?"

CHAP. II. The philosopher Yu said, "They are few who, being filial and fraternal, are fond of offending against their superiors. There have been none, who, not liking to offend against their superiors, have been fond of stirring up confusion."

CHAP. IV. The philosopher Tsang said, "I daily examine myself on three points—whether, in transacting business for others, I may have been not faithful—whether, in intercourse with friends, I may have been not sincere—whether I may have not mastered and practiced the instructions of my teacher."

CHAP. V. The Master said, "To rule a country of a thousand chariots, there must be reverent attention to business, and sincerity; economy in expenditure, and love for men; and the employment of the people at the proper seasons."

CHAP. VI. The Master said, "A youth, when at home, should be filial, and, abroad, respectful to his elders. He should be earnest and truthful. He should overflow in love to all, and cultivate the friendship of the good. When he has time and opportunity, after the performance of these things, he should employ them in polite studies."

CHAP. VII. Tsze-hsia said, "If a man withdraws his mind from the love of beauty, and applies it as sincerely to the love of the virtuous; if, in serving his parents, he can exert his utmost strength; if, in serving his prince, he can devote his life; if, in his intercourse with his friends, his words are sincere—although men say that he has not learned, I will certainly say that he has."

CHAP. VIII. "Hold faithfulness and sincerity as first principles."

"Have no friends not equal to yourself."

"When you have faults, do not fear to abandon them."

CHAP. X. Tsze-ch'in asked Tsze-kung, saying, "When our master comes to any country, he does not fail to learn all about its government. Does he ask his information? Or is it given to him?"

Tsze-kung said, "Our master is benign, upright, courteous, temperate, and complaisant, and thus he gets his information. The master's mode of asking information! Is it not different from that of other men?"

CHAP. XI. The Master said, "While a man's father is alive, look at the bent of his will; when his father is dead, look at his conduct. If for three years he does not alter from the way of his father, he may be called filial."

CHAP. XIII. The philosopher Yu said, "When agreements are made according to what is right, what is spoken can be made good. When respect is shown according to what is proper, one keeps far from shame and disgrace. When the parties upon whom a man leans are proper persons to be intimate with, he can make them his guides and masters."

CHAP. XIV. The Master said, "He who aims to be a man of complete virtue in his food does not seek to gratify his appetite, nor in his dwelling place does he seek the appliances of ease; he is earnest in what he is doing, and careful in his speech; he frequents the company of men of principle that he may be rectified—such a person may be said indeed to love to learn."

CHAP. XV. Tsze-kung said, "What do you pronounce concerning the poor man who yet does not flatter, and the rich man who is not proud?' The Master replied, 'They will do; but they are not equal to him, who, though poor, is yet cheerful, and to him, who, though rich, loves the rules of propriety."

Tsze-kung replied, "It is said in the *Book of Poetry*, 'As you cut and then file, as you carve and then polish.' – The meaning is the same, I apprehend, as that which you have just expressed."

The Master said, "With one like Ts'ze, I can begin to talk about the odes. I told him one point, and he knew its proper sequence."

CHAP. XVI. The Master said, "I will not be afflicted at men's not knowing me; I will be afflicted that I do not know men."

CORE BELIEFS

Confucius believed he was the purveyor of the wisdom of the ancients. From that wisdom he held that society consisted of five relationships: (1) husband and wife; (2) parents and children; (3) older and younger brother (or older and younger people); (4) rulers and subjects; and (5) friend and friend.

Confucian spirituality places strong emphasis on the role of family, calling for respect, piety and deference in familial interaction. These interactions are part and parcel of teachings on righteousness, ritual wisdom and faithfulness.

Confucius believed people must juggle their individual good with ultimate good. He thought that people are inherently good, but they need direction. If adhered to, direction leads to deeper virtue. He taught that individuals who put aside virtue for material pleasure make bad choices and go down an inferior path.

Confucius told his followers to have true compassion for one's own role and for the people one would encounter. He encouraged every person to live appropriately in his or her relationships. The essence of Confucianism is called *jen*, which literally means, "all the good things that happen when people meet," including hospitality and wishing them well.

Complimenting jen are five practices for good conduct: (1) *li*—respect for people in authority, whether a god, king or parent; (2) *hsiao*—familial love that includes distant relatives and even friends; (3) *yi*—mutual commitment among friends and, more generally, the cultivation of friendships; (4) *chung*—loyalty to the state; and (5) *chun-tzu*—an outgoing, generous, liberal presence.

In other traditions ritual means "to sacrifice" in a religious ceremony. In Confucianism the term is extended to include secular ceremonial behavior common to everyday life. Etiquette is codified and treated as an all-embracing system of norms. Confucius tried to revive the etiquette of earlier dynasties. Paradoxically, after Confucius' death his ideas became the standard of ritual behavior.

BRANCHES OF CONFUCIANISM

Confucianism as it exists today is derived primarily from the Neo-Confucian School led by Zhu Xi (1130–1200 C.E.) of the later Song Dynasty. He gave Confucianism renewed vigor. In later Chinese dynasties, the Neo-Confucian School of thought incorporated Taoist and Buddhist ideas to create a broader metaphysical system.

CONFUCIANISM IN THE MARKETPLACE

Confucianism in the Marketplace translates as four distinct concepts.

First, in order to organize a stable society, preference is given to the collective welfare, rather than to an individual's welfare. The reason is that people are interdependent. From the Confucian perspective, ethical business requires leaders to give thought to the well being of all people. If a company, or an entire country for that matter, were to benefit from "dishonesty," the act easily could be considered ethical because supposedly the whole community benefits.

Confucianism strongly emphasizes the network of obligations, duties and relationships binding an individual to the family, the community and the state. An individual's ethics must harmonize with that of the larger society in pursuit of a common good. Confucian business ethics combine both the public and the private realms in what is hoped to be a happy social whole.

Second, individuals with a Confucian worldview often avoid candor in order to "save face," as well as to ensure the avoidance of injury to the "faces" of others around them. This is in contrast to the Western path of excessive bluntness to gain prompt closure in a negotiation. As referenced earlier, this Confucian virtue is li, the sense of propriety required of all public and ceremonial action, whether simple or profound.

Third, business structures are extremely hierarchical and bureaucratic. Businesspeople are keenly sensitive to age, seniority, rank and status within organizations. They are more likely than their Western counterparts to accept the inequality in power and authority that exists in most organizations.

The five primary relationships—hsiao—underscore the hierarchical authority structures in Confucian businesses. What outsiders might call an inequality of power is thought of as not only a matter of relationship but also of custom or a ritual intrinsic to business decorum.

Fourth, Confucian thought lauds varying levels of honesty. *Analects* I 12 teaches, "Do not do to others what you would not like yourself," and Tseng Tzu wrote in *Analects* I 4: "Each day I examine myself in three ways. In doing things for others, have I been disloyal? In my interactions with friends, have I been untrustworthy? Have I not practiced what I have preached?"

In *Analects* II 3 Confucius wrote: "Lead the people with administrative injunctions and put them in their place with penal law, and they will avoid punishments but will be without a sense of shame. Lead them with excellence and put them in their place through roles and ritual practices, and in addition to developing a sense of shame, they will order themselves harmoniously."

The Confucian argument is that legal authorities administer punishments after anti-social actions, forcing people to generally behave well without understanding the reasons that they should. However, ritual patterns of behavior are internalized and exert their influence before actions are taken, allowing people to behave properly because they want to avoid losing face.

The reluctance to employ laws in a society where relationships are considered more important has given rise to corruption and nepotism. For example, the salaries of government officials in China historically have been far lower than the minimum required to raise a family. Solution: resort to bribery, kickbacks and nepotism to make up the difference. While there have been some practical methods to control and reduce corruption, many Chinese blame Confucianism for not providing the means to allow more significant reform to occur.

The downfall of Confucianism's strictly authoritarian social system is the lack of a guidance mechanism to judge whether a superior person is behaving appropriately, and when the line is crossed beyond which the duty of loyalty is no longer owed. In countries that follow Confucian thought, abuse of power continues until it becomes intolerable. Then the tyrant is overthrown.

The underlying value in Confucianism is social harmony based on the assumption that everyone tries his or her best. If people, especially those in leadership, do not try their best, there are no practical safeguards against negligence or misconduct.

REFERENCES AND FURTHER READING

Brooks, E. Bruce. *The Original Analects.* New York: Columbia University Press, 2001.

Canright, Robert E., Jr. *Achieve Lasting Happiness: Timeless Secrets to Transform Your Life.* Bloomington: Authorhouse, 2005.

Chan, Wing-Tsit. *A Source Book in Chinese Philosophy.* Princeton: Princeton University Press, 1969.

Confucius. *Confucius: The Analects.* New York: Penguin Classics, 1998.

Fingarette, Herbert. *Confucius: The Secular as Sacred (Religious Traditions of the World).* Prospect Heights: Waveland Press, 1998.

Freedman, Russell. *Confucius: The Golden Rule.* New York: Arthur A. Levine Books, 2002.

Waley, Arthur. *Three Ways of Thought in Ancient China.* Palo Alto, Stanford University Press, 1983.

CHAPTER 3
SHINTOISM

The heart of the person before you is a mirror.

See there your own.

Shinto saying

Shintoism is the world's fifteenth largest religion with some four million practitioners. It was at one time Japan's state religion. It emphasizes the worship of nature, ancestors, ancient heroes and the virtue of living with a "true heart." The guiding concept of Shinto is that a true heart is filled with sincerity and uprightness, and this is only possible through awareness of the divine. Shintoism's gods number 10 million. They are found in nature, honored in temples and makeshift shrines, and venerated as household gods.

HISTORY

A number of theories exist about the origins of Japanese Shintoism. Most scholars believe peoples from central Asia and Indonesia migrated to the Japanese Islands, bringing their beliefs with them. Japanese nationalists claim that Shintoism has always existed, arising from the ancient mists of the Jomon Age approximately 10,000 years ago.

More probable is that Shintoism developed during the Yayoi Period (300 B.C.E.–300 C.E.) via immigration from China and Korea. The agricultural and shamanistic ceremonies of these foreign lands were adapted to the new Japanese environment.

Some modern scholars assert that Shinto as presently practiced did not exist in the Jomon Age and should be more properly referred to as *kami* worship.

Shinto actually means "the way of the kami" or "divine way." It did not have a name until Chinese Buddhists began appearing around 500 C.E. To distinguish between the worship of the kami and the Buddha, the name Shinto was developed. It was not, however, until the late 12th Century C.E. that the term Shinto was used to refer to a specific body of religious ideas.

Shintoism is a form of animism that involves the worship of kami gods. Some kami are local and can be regarded as the spirit of a particular place. Others represent major natural objects and processes, e.g. Amaterasu, the sun goddess.

Several thousand years ago each Japanese tribe and area had its own collection of gods with no formal relationship among them. Following the ascendancy of the Yamato Kingdom around the 3rd to 5th Centuries C.E., the ancestral deities of the Emperor of Japan were given prominence over others. A story developed to explain this emergence, resulting in the myth found in the *Kojiki* (*Records of Ancient Matters* 712). Legend claimed that the Imperial line descended directly from the sun goddess herself.

Early ceremonies are thought to have been held outdoors in front of sacred rocks (*Iwakura*). The kami bore no physical image because they were conceived without form. After the arrival of Buddhism in the 6th Century C.E., the idea of building "houses" for the kami arose, and shrines were constructed for the first time. The earliest examples were built at Izumo in 659 C.E. and Ise in 691 C.E.

The introduction of the Ritsuryo System, based upon the Chinese system of order, in the late 7th and early 8th Centuries C.E. established in law the supremacy of the emperor and great nobles, as well as formalizing their relationship to major shrines and festivals. Although clan rivalry led to friction and fighting during the introduction of Buddhism, the worship of kami and the teachings of the Buddha soon settled into coexistence.

Over time the original nature-worshipping roots of Shintoism, while never lost entirely, became obsolete, and the kami took on more tangible and physical forms. The kami, though, are not transcendent deities in the usual religious sense. Although holy, they inhabit the same world as we do, make the same mistakes, and feel and think as humans would.

Following the Meiji Restoration, Shintoism was made the official religion of Japan, and in 1868 C.E. integration of Buddhist practices was made illegal. The arrival of Western military ideas and the subsequent collapse of the Shogunate convinced many Japanese that Shinto was an essential tool in unifying the nation around the emperor. It was therefore exported into territories taken by conquest, Hokkaido and Korea being primary examples.

A Ministry of Divinities was formed in 1871. Shinto shrines were divided into twelve levels with the Ise Shrine at the top and small sanctuaries in humble towns at the bottom. The following year the ministry was replaced with a new Ministry of Religion that was given the task of educating the population in moral virtue. Shinto priests were now nominated and organized by the state. They instructed the youth in a form of Shinto theology based on the official version of the divine origins of Japan and the emperor.

Shinto was increasingly used to promote nationalistic solidarity in Japan. In 1890 the "Imperial Prescript on Education" became law. Students were required to ritually recite its oath to offer themselves courageously to the state and to protect the Imperial Family with their own lives. The patriotic role of Shintoism was locked in mysticism and cultural introversion, which gave the Japanese government virtually unquestioned popular support for the invasions that precipitated World War II. Even when it was clear that Japan could not win, a large segment of the populace remained prepared to defend the emperor and their homeland to the death.

After Japan's unconditional surrender, the emperor issued a statement renouncing his claims to the status of "living god." After the war most Japanese people came to believe that excessive pride in the empire led to their defeat. As a result the devotion to Shintoism declined considerably while a number of new religions developed, many of them based upon the principles of Shinto or other Eastern and animistic religions.

Consequently Shintoism has reverted to the status of folk religion, culturally ingrained rather than politically enforced. In spite of its smaller base of followers, Shinto continues to serve as an important foundation of Japanese culture.

SACRED TEXTS

Shintoism does not have a sacred text *per se*. The works closest to being considered Shinto scripture are the *Kojiki (Records of Ancient Matters)* and *Nihongi (Chronicles of Japan)*. In addition to their role in Shinto tradition, these works offer historical information about Japan and examples of early Japanese literature.

SELECTED READINGS

VOL. I. PREFACE
I Asmara say:

Now when chaos had begun to condense, but force and form were not yet manifest, and there was naught named, naught done, who could know its shape? Nevertheless Heaven and Earth first parted, and the Three Deities performed the commencement of creation; the Passive and Active Essences then developed, and the Two Spirits became the ancestors of all things. Therefore did he enter obscurity and emerge into light, and the Sun and Moon were revealed by the washing of his eyes; he floated on and plunged into the seawater, and Heavenly and Earthly Deities appeared through the ablutions of his person. So in the dimness of the great commencement, we, by relying on the original teaching, learn the time of the conception of the earth and of the birth of islands; in the remoteness of the original beginning, we, by trusting the former sages, perceive the era of the genesis of Deities and of the establishment of men....

....In the august reign of the Heavenly Sovereign who governed the Eight Great Islands from the Great Palace of Kiyomihara at Asuka, the Hidden Dragon put on perfection, the Reiterated Thunder came at the appointed moment. Having heard a song in a dream, he felt that he should continue the succession; having reached the water at night, he knew that he should receive the inheritance. Nevertheless Heaven's time was not yet, and he escaped like the cicada to the Southern Mountains; both men and matters were favorable, and he marched like the tiger to the Eastern Land. Suddenly riding in the Imperial Palanquin, he forced his way across mountains and rivers: the Six Divisions rolled like thunder, the Three Hosts sped like lightning. The erect spears lifted up their might, and the bold warriors arose like smoke: the crimson flags glistened among the weapons, and the ill-omened crew were shattered like tiles. Or ere a day had elapsed, the evil influences were purified: forthwith were the cattle let loose and the horses given repose, as with shouts of victory they returned to the Flowery Summer; the flags were rolled up and the javelins put away, as with dances and chants they came to rest in the capital city....

....Hereupon the Heavenly Sovereign commanded, saying: "I hear that the chronicles of the emperors and likewise the original words in the possession of the various families deviate from exact truth, and are mostly amplified by empty falsehoods. If at the present time these imperfections be not amended, ere many years shall have elapsed, the purport of this, the great basis of the country, the grand foundation of the monarchy, will be destroyed. So now I desire to have the chronicles of the emperors selected and recorded, and the old words examined and ascertained, falsehoods being erased and the truth deter....

....Prostrate I consider how Her Majesty the Empress, having obtained Unity, illumines the empire, --being versed in the Triad, nourishes the people. Ruling from the Purple Palace, Her virtue reaches to the utmost limits of the horse's hoof-marks: dwelling amid the Sombre Retinue, Her influence illumines the furthest distance attained to by vessels' prows. The sun rises, and the brightness is increased; the clouds disperse, neither is there smoke. Never cease the historiographers from recording the good omens of connected stalks and double rice-ears; never for a single moon is the treasury without the tribute of continuous beacon-fires and repeated interpretations. In fame She must be pronounced superior to Bum-Mei, in virtue more eminent than Ten-Itsu....

...Altogether I have written Three Volumes, which I reverently and respectfully present. I Yasumaro, with true trembling and true fear, bow my head, bow my head.

Reverently presented by the Court Noble Futo no Yasumaro, an Officer of the Upper Division of the Fifth Rank and of the Fifth Order of Merit, on the 28th day of the first moon of the fifth year of Wa-dō.

[SECT. I—THE BEGINNING OF HEAVEN AND EARTH]
The names of the Deities that were born in the Plain of High Heaven when the Heaven and Earth began were the Deity Master-of-the-August-Centre-of-Heaven, next the High-August-Producing-Wondrous Deity,

next the Divine-Producing-Wondrous-Deity. These three Deities were all Deities born alone, and hid their persons. The names of the Deities that were born next from a thing that sprouted up like unto a reed-shoot when the earth, young and like unto floating oil, drifted about medusa-like, were the Pleasant-Reed-Shoot-Prince-Elder Deity, next the Heavenly-Eternally-Standing-Deity. These two Deities were likewise born alone, and hid their persons.

[SECT. XXIII—THE NETHER-DISTANT-LAND]

[The Deity Great-House-Prince spoke to him] saying: "Thou must set off to the Nether-Distant-Land where dwells His Impetuous-Mate-Augustness. That Great Deity will certainly counsel thee." So on his obeying her command and arriving at the august place of His Impetuous-Male-Augustness, the latter's daughter the Forward-Princess came out and saw him, and they exchanged glances and were married, and [she] went in again, and told her father, saying: "A very beautiful Deity has come." Then the Great Deity went out and looked, and said: 'This is the Ugly-Male-Deity-of-the-Reed-Plain," and at once calling him in, made him sleep in the snake-house. Hereupon his wife, Her Augustness the Forward-Princess, gave her husband a snake-scarf, saying: "When the snakes are about to bite thee, drive them away by waving this scarf thrice."

CORE BELIEFS

Shintoism is a form of animism, the attribution of a soul to plants, inanimate objects and natural phenomena, and may be regarded as a type of shamanist religion. Shinto beliefs are deeply embedded in the subconscious fabric of modern Japanese society. The afterlife is not a primary concern in Shinto, and much more emphasis is placed on fitting into this world as opposed to preparing for the next.

Shinto has no binding set of beliefs, no holiest place of worship, no person serving as holy leader and no defined set of prayers. Rather, Shinto is a collection of rituals and methods meant to mediate the relations of living humans to kami. The kami are born, live, die and are reborn like all other beings in the karmic cycle. These beliefs have evolved organically in Japan over a span of many centuries and have been influenced by Japan's contact with the religions of other nations, especially China.

The nearest equivalent to core beliefs are the Four Affirmations incorporated into the daily religious traditions of Shinto practitioners.

(1) Devotion to family and ancestral traditions.

(2) A reverence and love for all living and inanimate objects found in nature. Thus a waterfall, the moon, sand or merely an oddly shaped rock might be regarded as a kami. Kami also may be charismatic persons or abstractions such as growth and fertility.

(3) Ritual bathing to spiritually and physically cleanses oneself before entering a shrine to worship the kami.

(4) *Matsuri* or the worship and honoring of gods and ancestral spirits.

Proper observation of Shinto ritual is more important than whether one truly believes in the ritual. Therefore even practitioners of other religions may be venerated as kami after their deaths, the caveat being there are Shinto believers who wish them to be.

BRANCHES OF SHINTOISM

With the introduction of Buddhism and its absorption by the Imperial Court, it became necessary to distinguish between native Japanese beliefs and Buddhist teachings. Indeed, Shinto did not have a name until it had to be differentiated from Buddhism.

One Buddhist view of the Japanese kami explained them as supernatural beings still caught in the cycle of birth and rebirth. Buddhists believed that the kami played a special role in protecting their religion and allowing its teachings to flourish within Japan. Kukai, the founder of the True Word School of Buddhism in Japan, went further. He saw the kami as different embodiments of the Buddhas themselves.

Buddhism and Shinto coexisted and were amalgamated as the Shin-butsu Shugo. Kukai's synergetic views were widely held until the end of the Edo Period in the late 19th Century C.E. At that time Japan enacted a closed country policy, and that isolationism generated renewed interest in "Japanese studies" (*Kokugaku*).

Earlier in the 18th Century various Japanese scholars, in particular Motoori Norinaga (1730–1801 C.E.), tried to distinguish the "real" Shinto from various foreign influences. This attempt was largely unsuccessful.

To understand the different focuses of emphasis within Shinto, it is important to designate how Shinto is structured.

(1) Shrine Shinto, the oldest and most prevalent of the Shinto types, has always been a part of Japan's history and constitutes the main current of Shinto tradition. The Ise Shrine, Shinto's most sacred site, is considered too important to preserve and is torn down every 20 years. Shinto priests model this demolition on nature. They then replace the shrine with a new one, a re-creation rather than a replica. It contains three legendary items dating back 2,000 years—a mirror, a string of jewels and a sword.

(2) Sect Shinto is comprised of thirteen groups formed during the 19th Century. They do not have shrines but conduct religious activities in meeting halls. Shinto sects include the mountain-worship sects that venerate mountains like Mt. Fuji, faith-healing sects, purification sects, Confucian sects and Revival Shinto sects. Konkokyo, Tenrikyo and Kurozumikyo, although operating separately from modern Shinto, are considered forms of Sect Shinto.

(3) Folk Shinto includes the numerous but fragmented folk beliefs in deities and spirits. Practices include divination, spirit possession and shamanic healing. Some of these practices are adopted from Taoism, Buddhism or Confucianism, and others come from ancient local traditions.

(4) State Shinto was the result of the downfall of the Shogunate. Reformers attempted to purify Shinto by purging many Buddhist and Confucian ideas, thus emphasizing the divinity of the emperor. Af-

ter Japan's defeat in World War II, State Shinto was abolished, and the emperor was forced to renounce his divinity. Some Shinto practices and teachings, once given prominence during the war, are neither taught nor practiced today. Others remain as secular activities engrained in the culture but disembodied from religious origins.

SHINTOISM IN THE MARKETPLACE

It is difficult to distinguish between the culture of Japanese business ethics in general and distinctly Shinto business ethics because each is so circularly tied to the other.

Speaking of all matters, the Oracle of Amaterasu at the Kotai Shrine says: "If you plot and connive to deceive people, you may fool them for a while, and profit thereby, but you will without fail be visited by divine punishment. To be utterly honest may have the appearance of inflexibility and self-righteousness, but in the end, such a person will receive the blessings of sun and moon. Follow honesty without fail."

In the specific matter of commerce, Shintoism translates as three distinct concepts—diligent effort, group primacy and reciprocity in relationships.

Diligence is the first principle. Members of Japanese society often feel compelled to work hard because, by doing so, they unify their individual spirits with the larger cosmos. This gives workers either a feeling of being at peace with the world or the hope that they can come to that peace if they work harder.

This same metaphysical process is strong in the macro-universe of Japanese business. The secular interpretation is that Japanese ethical norms assume that people will work tirelessly to contribute to the greater causes of their companies. The work ethic is at once an expression of religion and a process of self-actualization. Through the sacrifice of diligent work, the individual can connect himself with the greater, pooled life force and comply with the ethical expectations of society.

The second principle is the group. This orientation profoundly affects Japanese society and leaves a deep imprint on business ethics. In

Japan workers are expected to subordinate themselves to their companies, and companies are expected to subordinate themselves to the nation. Each group owes deference and allegiance to the next larger group in the chain. If a sub-group violates the expectations inherent in this hierarchy, it will be ridiculed or punished.

From a Western perspective the group ethic can create problems. If a worker has personal concerns regarding a new policy, he or she is likely to refrain from expressing an opinion. The Japanese word for "economy" (*keizai*) is derived from a set of words meaning, "to rule society and save people." The melding of ruling and saving is so strong in Japan that workers are expected to exhibit total obedience to their managers. Submission and inaction may perpetuate management's making unethical decisions or just plain stupid ones. Further, since many workers rely on the moral judgment of their superiors, they don't feel a strong responsibility to think about ethical behavior.

It also must be noted that Japanese group ethics apply only to groups inside Japanese society. Workers or managers do not feel compelled to uphold native standards when dealing with "alien" groups. That is to say, rival corporations, foreign nationals or different countries. Such a dichotomy between the value of things Japanese and non-Japanese provides a rationale for behaviors that outsiders consider amoral.

The third principle is reciprocity. The Japanese believe that long-term, give-and-take relationships are the hallmark of a harmonious society. That makes relationships a key element in business ethics. Business relationships in Japan require participants (firms, employees, government, society, etc.) to strike a balance between benefits and sacrifices.

Participants are expected to work diligently and rationally to create mutually beneficial business transactions. If one participant shirks his responsibility or otherwise fails to provide his expected contribution, the transgressor will be ostracized.

Reciprocal business relationships in Japan can best be understood as a series of revolving "ethical debts." A sacrifice by entity A incurs a sacrifice by entity B that incurs a sacrifice by entity C, *ad infinitum*. If a company or institution does not fulfill its obligations to its stakeholders or business partners, it violates the ethics of reciprocity.

An excellent example of the ethics of reciprocity can be seen in the actions of Japanese executives during poor business conditions. While many Western executives might lay off employees during a recession or when sales are down, Japanese executives do everything in their power to maintain their employees' jobs. Japanese executives will reduce their own pay, sell assets, cut wages, and/or reduce dividends before they will lay off workers.

The executives believe the company owes workers the obligation of employment in return for their allegiance and hard work. The workers recognize this sacrifice and thus push themselves to work harder and more efficiently. By attempting to balance the benefits and sacrifices in such a manner, both parties comply with the ethics of reciprocity.

Many Japanese managers question Western motives of putting shareholders' earnings as a first priority and then engaging in downsizing, mergers and acquisitions. In the Japanese mind, employees and companies are inextricably linked. They are mutually dependent and must work together in reciprocal business relationships to achieve long-term success. From the Japanese perspective, "value-enhancing" policies and actions commonly practiced in the West are myopic and unethical.

REFERENCES AND FURTHER READING

Capaldi, Nicholas. *Business and Religion: A Clash of Civilizations? (Conflicts and Trends in Business Ethics)*. Salem: M&M Scrivener Press, 2005.

De Bary, William Theodore. *Sources of Japanese Tradition, Vol. 2*. New York: Columbia University Press, 1964.

Fukami, Toshu. *Successful Business Management through Shinto*. Lincoln: iUniverse, 1999.

Littleton, C. Scott. *Shinto and the Religions of Japan*. New York: Oxford University Press USA, 2002.

Littleton, C. Scott. *Understanding Shinto: Origins, Beliefs, Practices, Festivals, Spirits, Sacred Places*. London: Duncan Baird Publishers, 2002.

Ono, Sokyo. Shinto: *The Kami Way*. Boston: Tuttle Publishing, 2004.

Tsunoda, Ryusaku. *Sources of Japanese Tradition, Vol. 1*. New York: Columbia University Press, 1964.

PART THREE

◉

RELIGIONS ORIGINATING IN INDIA

CHAPTER 4

BUDDHISM

*Hurt not others in ways that
you yourself would find hurtful.*

Udanavargu 5:18, Tibetan Dhammapada, 1983

With some 376 million followers, Buddhism is the world's sixth largest religion. The founder was Siddhartha Gautama. Twenty-seven centuries ago he turned his back on comfort and privilege to pursue the meaning of life. He became known as the "The Enlightened One," or the Buddha, and taught his followers the cause of suffering and the way to end it.

The main tenant of Buddhism is that death is only a transition for each life continuing in some other form—human, divine or animal. The form depends upon *karma*, or the results of behavior in the last life.

Life's biggest problem, no matter what the form, is suffering. By advancing on a path to enlightenment, suffering is overcome. Enlightenment is the ability to extinguish the flame of wanting and to cut any attachment to self. Once wanting is dampened and attachment severed, Nirvana is achieved. Nirvana is the ultimate state of being in which there is no more suffering, making further rebirth unnecessary.

When used in a broad sense, a Buddha is any individual who discovers the true nature of reality through years of spiritual study, investigation of the myriad religious practices of his time and meditation. This transformational discovery is called *bodhi* or awakening or enlightenment. Therefore any person who awakes from the "sleep of ignorance" by understanding the true nature of reality is called a Buddha.

One becomes a Buddha through the study of Siddhartha's words, which are called *dharma*, not to be confused with another definition of dharma that refers to the underlying order in nature and humans in response to that. In addition, one puts these words into practice through the leading of a virtuous life in order to purify the mind. The aim of Buddhist practice is to end the stress of existence. The dharma states, "I teach one thing and one thing only: suffering and the end of suffering."

Practitioners of Buddhism follow the Four Noble Truths, the Eightfold Path and the Middle Way. Through them, practitioners eventually end ignorance and unhappiness, attaining the liberation of Nirvana.

Most Buddhists recognize the existence of supernatural god-like beings, but adherents do not believe in an omnipotent creator. All Buddhists recognize a transcendent truth that some perceive as a "Buddha Nature" infusing all things.

HISTORY

Buddhism was an outgrowth of Hinduism that shaped the background and early years of Buddhism's revered founder. Siddhartha Gautama, the son of a wealthy and influential North Indian nobleman, lived around 563–483 B.C.E. Tradition says that Siddhartha's mother died at his birth, and a prophet predicted shortly thereafter that the baby Siddhartha would become either a great king or a great holy man. His father, in an attempt to make sure that his son would follow in his footsteps, made certain that Siddhartha never had any dissatisfaction with life and therefore would forsake a spiritual path. Siddhartha was raised in a palace and was carefully isolated from sad, sick and dying people.

But at the age of 21 Siddhartha came across what has become known as the Four Passing Sights. An old crippled man, a sick man, a decaying corpse and a wandering holy man. The four sights led Siddhartha to the realization that birth, old age, sickness and death come to everyone. From this realization came "The Great Renunciation," in which the young man of privilege left it all—rank, caste, and his wife and child—to become a wandering holy man in search of the deepest meaning of life.

Siddhartha tried meditation with two hermits, began training in Hindu ascetics, and practiced techniques of physical and mental austerity. He was troubled with many unanswered questions. Leaving behind Hinduism, he and a small group of companions set out to take their austerities even further.

After discarding asceticism to concentrate on meditation, Siddhartha discovered what Buddhists call the Middle Way—a path of moderation between extremes of self-indulgence and self-mortification.

To strengthen his body, he accepted some buttermilk from a passing village girl. Then he sat under a bodhi tree and vowed never to arise until he had found the truth. Siddhartha apparently found what he was looking for and, as the Enlightened One, he preached what has become known as Buddhism for the next 45 years. The Buddha founded two monastic communities of monks and nuns who continued his teaching after his death.

According to tradition, the Buddha once helped solve the problem of grief for a woman whose son had just died. She came to the Buddha and asked him to comfort her. He put a tiny mustard seed in her hand and told her to collect one mustard seed from every one of her neighbors but only if they had never lost a loved one to death. She returned later with the same mustard seed and the comforting awareness that every person has been touched by death.

Siddhartha himself died in the town of Kushinagara of food poisoning from a meal of bad pork that a blacksmith gave him. His body was cremated. His ashes and possibly other sacred relics were allegedly given to various temples or buried in religious monuments called *stupas*. Visiting the Buddha's ashes has since become an important pilgrimage for Buddhists.

Buddhism spread throughout the Indian subcontinent in the five centuries following the Buddha's death, and into Central, Southeast and East Asia over the following two millennia.

SACRED TEXTS

The Tripitaka is a collection of Buddhist scriptures compiled between 500 B.C.E. and 45 B.C.E. *The Tripitaka* contains three divisions or "baskets." Three versions survive. The first is in the Pali Language and is used by Southern Buddhists. There are two Mahayana versions in Chinese and Tibetan, and they are used by Northern Buddhists.

The Tripitaka baskets include:

(1) *Vinaya Pitaka* which codifies the rules, regulations and disciplinary conduct for life in a Buddhist monastery.

(2) *Sutta Pitaka* is a compilation of the stories of the life and teachings (dharma) of the first Buddha.

(3) *Abhidhamma Pitaka* is an ancient dictionary that defines religious terms and discusses elements of existence and casual relationships.

Additionally, Theravada Buddhists look at the *Dhammapada*, which is an anthology of Buddhist proverbs and teachings, as a sacred text. Its message defines the right path to wisdom in a transitory world.

Mahayana Buddhists include in their canon later books not recognized as authoritative by southern Buddhists.

(1) *The Siksha Samukhya* presents the sutras (the scriptural words of Buddha) written by Santideva who, like Buddha, renounced the old life. Santideva embraced the Mahayana form of Buddhism. For this reason his work has limited sacred value to the Theravada branch.

(2) Mahayana texts include the *Tibetan Book of the Dead*, the *Translation of the Word of the Buddha*, the *Translation of the Treatises*, the *Great Scripture Store (Chinese)*, the *Lotus Sutra* and the *Heart Sutra*.

SELECTED READINGS

The following texts are taken from the *Dhammapada*.

Chapter I

The Twin-Verses

All that we are is the result of what we have thought: it is founded on our thoughts, it is made up of our thoughts. If a man speaks or acts with an evil thought, pain follows him, as the wheel follows the foot of the ox that draws the carriage.

All that we are is the result of what we have thought: it is founded on our thoughts, it is made up of our thoughts. If a man speaks or acts with a pure thought, happiness follows him, like a shadow that never leaves him.

"He abused me, he beat me, he defeated me, he robbed me," in those who harbor such thoughts hatred will never cease.

"He abused me, he beat me, he defeated me, he robbed me," in those who do not harbor such thoughts hatred will cease.

For hatred does not cease by hatred at any time: hatred ceases by love, this is an old rule.

The world does not know that we must all come to an end here; but those who know it, their quarrels cease at once.

He who lives looking for pleasures only, his senses uncontrolled, immoderate in his food, idle, and weak, Mara (the tempter) will certainly overthrow him, as the wind throws down a weak tree.

He who lives without looking for pleasures, his senses well controlled, moderate in his food, faithful and strong, him Mara will certainly not overthrow, any more than the wind throws down a rocky mountain....

....The follower of the law, even if he can recite only a small portion (of the law), but, having forsaken passion and hatred and foolishness, possesses true knowledge and serenity of mind, he, caring for nothing in this world or that to come, has indeed a share in the priesthood.

Chapter II

On Earnestness

Earnestness is the path of immortality (Nirvana), thoughtlessness the path of death. Those who are in earnest do not die, those who are thoughtless are as if dead already.

Those who are advanced in earnestness, having understood this clearly, delight in earnestness, and rejoice in the knowledge of the Ariyas (the elect).

These wise people, meditative, steady, always possessed of strong powers, attain to Nirvana, the highest happiness....

....Fools follow after vanity, men of evil wisdom. The wise man keeps earnestness as his best jewel.

Follow not after vanity, nor after the enjoyment of love and lust! He who is earnest and meditative, obtains ample joy.

When the learned man drives away vanity by earnestness, he, the wise, climbing the terraced heights of wisdom, looks down upon the fools, serene he looks upon the toiling crowd, as one that stands on a mountain looks down upon them that stand upon the plain.

Chapter IX

Evil

If a man would hasten towards the good, he should keep his thought away from evil; if a man does what is good slothfully, his mind delights in evil.

If a man commits a sin, let him not do it again; let him not delight in sin: pain is the outcome of evil.

If a man does what is good, let him do it again; let him delight in it: happiness is the outcome of good.

Even an evildoer sees happiness as long as his evil deed has not ripened; but when his evil deed has ripened, then does the evildoer see evil.

Even a good man sees evil days, as long as his good deed has not ripened; but when his good deed has ripened, then does the good man see happy days.

Let no man think lightly of evil, saying in his heart, It will not come nigh unto me. Even by the falling of water-drops a water-pot is filled; the fool becomes full of evil, even if he gather it little by little.

Let no man think lightly of good, saying in his heart, it will not come nigh unto me. Even by the falling of water-drops a water-pot is filled; the wise man becomes full of good, even if he gather it little by little....

....Some people are born again; evildoers go to hell; righteous people go to heaven; those who are free from all worldly desires attain Nirvana.

CORE BELIEFS

Siddhartha was not the only Buddha, but he is by far the most important. He taught his followers to seek release from their stresses in life by looking inside themselves. A common Buddhist saying is, "Be a lamp unto your own feet." You do not need an outside light or a transcendent deity to lead you to enlightenment.

Enlightenment ultimately means Nirvana, the state in which all desire is extinguished, and realization of self does not exist. Nirvana is neither positive nor negative in a moral sense, and although it is viewed as a happy existence, there is no expectation for feelings of joy. A Buddhist who has attained Nirvana has escaped the world of cause-and-effect, and is free from the cycle of birth and rebirth.

Falling short of Nirvana, a Buddhist is subject to *karma* or the moral and spiritual consequences of his actions. If the sum of deeds is more good than bad, the Buddhist moves forward toward happiness, perfection and enlightenment. Conversely, if karma is bad, they return to a former state of existence or to a lower life form. Extremely special people who have made it to Nirvana return as enlightened souls called *bodhisattva*, sometime lamas, who teach humanity about the path to freedom.

There are four stages in the Buddhist life:

(1) The "Stream-Entrant" who catches only a glimpse of Nirvana in the teaching of the Buddha.

(2) The "Once-Returned" who is destined to be reborn into this physical world before experiencing full Nirvana.

(3) The "Never-Returned" who has an even deeper knowledge of Nirvana that assures that he or she will not be reborn.

(4) The "Worthy-One" who is completely free of desire. This person has experienced Nirvana and will know it fully at death when all matter, sensations, perceptions, mental cognition and consciousness disappear forever.

Advancing through these stages requires intimacy with Four Nobel Truths, The Eightfold Path and The Three Jewels.

Four Noble Truths

(1) All human life is about suffering. Nothing lasts—not happiness, not sadness, not things good or bad. From the moment we are born, our bodies start to die and decay. The world is an illusion. There is no self, no permanence and things that we think are necessary are fleeting. This state of temporary being is what causes sorrow and suffering.

(2) The causes of suffering are desire and ignorance. Being ignorant of the true nature of things, people always strive to obtain something they think they want, the absence of what is wanted causes pain.

(3) Suffering will finally stop when we attain Nirvana, a state of being in which we understand the true nature of existence and no longer feel desire.

(4) The way to attain Nirvana is with the Eightfold Path. The Buddhist who lives this middle path accepts the truths as Buddhism outlines them, and avoids killing, stealing, lying, abusing sex and taking any intoxicants.

The Eightfold Path

In order to fully understand the Four Noble Truths and investigate whether they were in fact true, Buddha recommended that a path be followed that has eight attributes.

(1) The Right View by realizing the Four Noble Truths.

(2) The Right Intention by commitment to mental and ethical growth in moderation.

(3) The Right Speech by which one's words do not cause harm, do not exaggerate and are truthful.

(4) The Right Action by behaving wholesomely and not harming others.

(5) The Right Livelihood in which one's job does not harm oneself or others.

(6) The Right Effort to keep improving.

(7) Right Mindfulness to cultivate the mental ability to see things clearly for what they are.

(8) The Right Concentration to get to where one reaches enlightenment and the ego has disappeared.

Some Buddhists say that The Eightfold Path is a progression of stages through which the practitioner moves, the culmination of one stage leading to the beginning of another. Others say that all stages of the Path require simultaneous development.

The Three Jewels

Acknowledging the Four Noble Truths and making the first step in The Eightfold Path require a foundation of religious practice; otherwise known as Buddhism's Three Jewels.

(1) The Buddha, or the Awakened One, is a title for those who attain enlightenment similar to the first Buddha.

(2) The dharma is the teachings or law as expounded by the Buddha. The Buddha presented himself as a model and beseeched his followers to have faith in his example as a human who escaped the pain and danger of existence. The dharma provides guidelines for the alleviation of suffering and the attainment of enlightenment. Dharma also means the law of nature based on behavior and its consequences.

(3) The *Sangha* literally means "group" or "congregation," but when it is used in Buddhist teachings it refers to two specific kinds of groups. These are a community either of Buddhist monastics or of people who have attained at least the first stage of Awakening, i.e., ones who have entered the stream to enlightenment. As Buddhism migrated to the West, a new usage of the word emerged: a meditation group or any sort of spiritual community. Whatever the degree of enlightenment, the Sangha is supposed to preserve the authentic teachings of the Buddha and to present examples that his teachings are attainable.

Many Buddhists believe that there is no otherworldly salvation from one's karma. The suffering caused by the karmic effects of previous thoughts, words and deeds can be alleviated by following the Four Noble Truths and The Eightfold Path. The Buddha of some Mahayana sutras, such as the Lotus Sutra, the Angulimaliya Sutra and the Nirvana Sutra, also teach that powerful sutras can, through the very act of their being heard or recited, wipe out great swathes of negative karma.

Buddha originally spoke the Four Noble Truths, not as religious or philosophical dialogue, but in the form of the common medical prescription of his time. Buddha said that followers should use his teachings only if they help. He compared worrying about things such as an afterlife to ministering to a person who has been shot with an arrow by contemplating who made the arrow, rather than removing it.

Buddhism has a variety of sects, nearly all of which agree on the Four Noble Truths. One of the areas of difference is the Hindu caste system. Some sects accept it as a social reality but reject it as way of indicating that any person is superior to another. Other sects reject the caste system entirely. Regardless of the sect, the unifying belief is that people of any class can achieve Nirvana if they live in an enlightened way.

BRANCHES OF BUDDHISM

Buddhism has two primary schools of thought. The first, Theravada Buddhism, is known as the "Doctrine of the Elders," and is practiced in Burma, Sri Lanka, Thailand, Cambodia, Vietnam and Laos. Because Theravada historically dominated southern Asia, it is sometimes called "Southern Buddhism." Theravada Buddhism is the sect most popular in the West. This school emphasizes the role of the individual in transforming the universe. The practitioner must gain wisdom that gives insights into the nature of reality and the causes of anxiety and suffering, and reveals that everything is an illusion.

The second school of thought, Mahayana Buddhism, is practiced in Nepal, China, Tibet, Mongolia, Korea and Japan. Mahayana Buddhism is also known as "Northern Buddhism" because it migrated northwards from India into China, Tibet, Japan and Korea. It postulates that we are not alone in this world but are helped in our spiritual journey by bodhi-sattvas. A bodhisattva is a semi-divine being who voluntarily renounces Nirvana to return to the earth to help others attain enlightenment.

In Theravada Buddhism a bodhisattva is regarded differently, namely as someone who has yet to reach Nirvana but is on the road and can teach others the way.

The goal of every Buddhist is to be a person of compassion. This quality is not automatic but must be cultivated by connecting with a bodhisattva.

Theravada Buddhism

Theravada Buddhism is known as the smaller vehicle of the two main branches of Buddhism because not many people want to walk down the path of celibacy and poverty. Most monks and nuns live in a community and give up almost everything except a robe, a belt, a begging bowl, and a needle and thread. They eat but one meal a day.

Theravada Buddhism came into existence as a reform movement against some aspects of Hindu tradition. It sought to give an equal voice to women, wipe out the inequalities of the caste system and do away with the concept of reincarnation (*samsara*). The movement did not meet its goals, but it did develop into a religious tradition that venerated the words of Siddhartha Gautama.

Mahayana Buddhism

Mahayana Buddhism is known as the greater vehicle and embraces the majority of Buddhist followers today.

In his lifetime Siddhartha did not answer several philosophical questions. Is the world eternal or non-eternal? Finite or infinite? What is the nature of unity? How is the body separated from the self? What is it like for a person to attain the complete non-existence of Nirvana? Mahayana commentators explain that the Buddha remained silent on these and other questions because they distract from practical activity for realizing enlightenment.

In numerous Mahayana *sutras* and *tantras*, the Buddha stresses dharma. The Buddha himself cannot be truly understood with the ordinary rational mind. Both the Buddha and reality (ultimately they are one) transcend all worldly logic. What is urged is study, mental and moral self-improvement and veneration of the sutras that are as fingers pointing to "the moon of Truth." It is necessary, however, that a practitioner of Mahayana Buddhism let go of reason.

Offshoots

Theravada and Mahayana Buddhism are only two of thousands of sects within Buddhism. Some of the better known include Zen, Shingon, Pure Land, Soka Gakkai and Lamaism.

Zen Buddhism, a Japanese form that became a significant spiritual movement in the 12th Century C.E., is perhaps the best-known sect. It promotes sudden enlightenment as opposed to the more traditional Buddhist view that enlightenment comes gradually.

Lamaism is the Tibetan form of Buddhism that is also practiced in Mongolia. Lamas, who are teachers and priests, provide guidance. The most famous is the exiled Dahli Lama whose role in Tibet was meant to be both a sectarian leader and a priestly leader.

BUDDHISM IN THE MARKETPLACE

The different schools of Buddhism generally align in terms of what the lay Buddhist should do to cultivate good business practices. Buddhism in the marketplace translates into adhering to the Five Precepts. The Five Precepts are training rules for life. Breaking any of them results in bad karma.

(1) Avoid taking the life of beings. This precept applies to all living beings, not just humans, because killing something as lowly as a bug

could mean killing your Uncle Ernie who died last year and was reincarnated as that bug.

(2) Avoid taking things not given. This precept goes further than mere stealing. People should avoid taking anything not intended for them.

(3) Avoid sensual misconduct. This precept is often misinterpreted as relating only to sexual misconduct, but it admonishes overindulgence in any sensual pleasure such as gluttony.

(4) Avoid false speech. This precept covers lying and deceiving, slander and gossip, any speech not beneficial to the welfare of others.

(5) Avoid substances that cause intoxication and heedlessness. This precept does not imply any intrinsic evil in, say, alcohol, but a Buddhist should infer that indulgence in drink could cause the breaking of the other four precepts.

The Buddha's advice to a group of lay people on how to live a good life was: (1) be energetic and diligent in performing your job; (2) take care of your wealth; (3) associate with true friends, meaning wise and virtuous people who will help you and protect you, and guide you in the path of morality and religion; and (4) do not spend more than your means allow, but do not be tight-fisted either, clinging to your wealth.

Charity and generosity are encouraged. The wealthy in particular have an obligation to help the poor. The word for a Buddhist monk, *bhikshu* (or for nun, *bhiksuni*) means "beggar." The traditional giving of alms to the Sangha, the community of monks, is as old as Buddhism itself. Every morning people place food into the begging bowls of monks.

In an ideal world Buddhist practice would lead to completely ethical business behavior. But as the Buddha himself taught, people are motivated by greed, hatred and delusion, even Buddhists.

REFERENCES AND FURTHER READING

Harvey, Peter. *An Introduction to Buddhist Ethics: Foundations, Values and Issues.* Cambridge: Cambridge University Press, 2000.

Heine, Steven. *White Collar Zen: Using Zen Principles to Overcome Obstacles and Achieve Your Career Goals.* New York: Cambridge University Press USA, 2005.

Herman, Stewart W. *Spiritual Goods: Faith Traditions and the Practice of Business.* Charlottesville: Philosophy Documentation Center, 2001.

Larkin, Geraldine A. *Building a Business the Buddhist Way: A Practitioner's Guidebook.* Berkeley: Celestial Arts, 1999.

Metcalf, Franz. *What Would Buddha Do at Work? 101 Answers to Workplace Dilemmas.* Berkeley: Seastone Press, 2001.

Richmond, Lewis. *Work as a Spiritual Practice: A Practical Buddhist Approach to Inner Growth and Satisfaction on the Job.* New York: Broadway Books, 2000.

Witten, Dona, and Akong Tulku Rinpoche. *Enlightened Management: Bringing Buddhist Principles to Work.* South Paris: Park Street Press, 1999.

CHAPTER 5

HINDUISM

Let no man do to another that which

would be repugnant to himself.

Mahabharata book 5, chapter 49, verse 57

Hinduism is the world's oldest known religion and the fourth largest with over 900 million followers. It is the main religion of India where 96% of its practitioners live, but it is the Himalayan kingdom of Nepal that is the world's only Hindu nation. Hinduism is the world's most closed religion. You are not only born a Hindu but also positioned into one of its four castes, the status or stigma thereof permanent for at least a lifetime.

Hindus believe in the *Brahman*, an eternal, infinite principal that has no beginning, has no end, and is the source and substance of all existence. A Westerner with a Judeo-Christian background might incorrectly compare Brahman to God, but Hollywood is more on point with The Force in *Star Wars*. Drop the "n" in Brahman and you get Brahma, a *deva* or god that is born without a mother. Brahma created the universe, but he is not supreme, not Brahman.

Hindus believe in transmigration, the soul passing into another body at death, and in reincarnation, a cycle of death and rebirth. Hindus believe in karma, the idea that your actions in one life have a direct effect on the events in your next life. To Hindus salvation comes when you are finally released from the cycle of death and rebirth.

Many who practice within the Hindu faith view suffering as purposeful. The goal of Hindus is to find release from the cycle of birth-death-rebirth that continues until a person can be freed from desires that keeps the cycle going. Once this recycling has ended, a person's soul can return to Brahman.

The Hindu idea of heaven is contained in the word *moksha*, meaning freedom or salvation. To the Hindu, moksha is the annihilation of individuality, like a drop of water dissolving in the ocean. Hindus use yoga and meditation to strive for moksha.

HISTORY

Hinduism, which dates from about 4000 B.C.E., is deeply connected to the culture of India, has no known founder and does not reflect the teachings of any particular prophet or holy person.

The roots of modern Hinduism go back as far as 3000–1000 B.C.E. according to Vedic traditions. Historically, Hindus can be referred to as the successors of Vedic Aryans and other tribes of India. From their descendants comes a popular name for India—Hindustan, meaning the land of Hindus. The complex, fully formed Hinduism of today did not emerge until these Vedic traditions interacted with the shamanistic movements of Buddhism and Jainism, both of which started as offshoots of Hinduism.

Sometimes the claim is made that Hinduism is a monotheistic religion because it accepts that all things are part of the divine force called Brahman. More accurately, Hinduism should be characterized as polytheistic because it embraces other religions as true expressions of Brahmanic principle. The incongruities that other religions may have with Brahman, and the outright opposition that some faiths have with others, which at times extends to Hinduism, make no difference to Hindus. One small factor of polytheism can be the obvious worship of many gods, but the more basic characteristic is that many paths exist, and no one truth overrides another.

Therefore it is perfectly acceptable for Hindus to worship, for example, Allah, the God of monotheistic Islam. In Hindu temples often displayed are a myriad pictures of different gods, some which are traditionally Hindu and others Eastern or Western. Except for the adoration of deities, Hinduism's inclusion of many paths has much in common with the relativistic moral philosophy of Secular Postmodernism.

Hindu scriptures insist that Brahman cannot be described in words but can be understood only through direct experience. Nevertheless, Hindu sages have endeavored to depict the nature of Brahman. These attempts make up a large portion of the Hindu scriptures, particularly in the ancient Vedic texts known as the *Upanishads*.

Brahma comes from the same root word as Brahman, but Brahma is merely the creator. The god Shiva is the destroyer, and Vishnu is the affirmer. Hindus also worship the goddess Kali, the wife of Shiva, who is the most terrifying goddess. The Hindu religion includes hundreds of other gods and goddesses that divide responsibility for all the parts of life in the world.

Hindu gods are not jealous, fighting gods, and they do not demand exclusive reverence. Because of this openness, Hindus seek to include people of other faiths. However, a typical Hindu generally chooses one God for personal devotion (Krishna, Rama, Shiva or Kali are among the top choices) and cultivates devotion to that chosen form while at the same time respecting others. Occasionally, depending on circumstances or need, most Hindus will worship deities other than their top choice. Nonetheless, they believe that all of these gods are part of one divine essence that permeates the universe. It is not expected for a Hindu to know about every god, and it is considered impossible to worship every one.

SACRED TEXTS

Hinduism's sacred texts include the *vedas*, *Upanishads*, *Bhagavad-Gita*, *Mahabharata* and *Ramayana*. These scriptures are divided into two categories.

(1) *Shruti* means that which is not heard. Shruti literature came from sages who are called *rishis*. They are said to have written down the texts without any changes whatsoever from their eternal form. Texts, then, were revealed as opposed to being created by human authors. The vedas, including the *Upanishads*, are the most important examples of shruti.

(2) *Smriti* is that which is remembered. Smriti literature includes stories, legends and laws written down but not specifically revealed. The Smriti have come to represent an oral tradition of law and social customs in Hinduism. The three most important works of Smriti literature are the *Mahabharata*, the *Bhagavad-Gita* and the *Ramayana*.

Of the four works under the second heading, the two most widely read are the *Bhagavad-Gita*, which explains creation, the deities, and the connection between humans and the divine; and the *Upanishads* that gives spiritual advice to believers.

Of the four official *Vedas* under the first heading, the oldest and most prominent is the *Rig-Veda*, or songs of knowledge. The *Rig-Veda* contains more than 1,000 hymns. In general each hymn is addressed to a specific god such as Indra, the warrior who overcame the power of evil, or Agni, the god of fire, who linked earth and heaven.

The Aryans, a conquering people from the north, brought the Vedic literature with them. The *Rig-Veda* teaches that life is illusory, fleeting and has no meaning without sacrifice.

The *Rig-Veda* also introduces the most pervasive social element of Hindu tradition—the caste system.

(1) *Brahmin* (from the same root as Brahman and Brahma) are priests and scholars.

(2) *Ksatriya* are warriors and rulers.

(3) *Vaisya* are trades people, merchants and farmers.

(4) *Sudra* are the laborers and serfs, artisans and slaves.

Later another group, the Unscheduled Caste, was introduced. More popularly, its members were known as Untouchables.

In addition to the *Rig-Vedas*, the other *Vedas* are:

(1) The *Sama Veda* concentrates on the divine chants.

(2) The *Yajur Veda* speaks of the sacrificial rituals.

(3) The *Atharva Veda* focuses on the incarnations.

The Upanishads

The *Upanishads*, known as the mystery writings, are also classified as Vedic literature. Written about 600 B.C.E., they recount the oral teachings of the Hindu sages that went back to around 1000 B.C.E. The *Upanishads* are called *Vedanta* (end of the vedas) and is the central theological teaching of Hinduism.

The *Upanishads* deal with the nature of ultimate reality. They speculate on the relationship between the individual soul (*atman*) and the soul of the ultimate reality and god of the universe, Brahman. The nature of reincarnation and the nature of creation are primary themes of the *Upanishads*.

The Mahabharata

The *Mahabharata*, often called the fifth Veda, is huge epic of 110,000 couplets that recount the war between the Pandavas, a family that symbolizes the spirits of goodness, and the Kauravas who symbolize evil. Unlike the other *Vedas* that primarily focus on the importance of sacrificial ritual, the *Mahabharata* promotes *bhakti*, devotion to the lord. Unlike other vedas, the *Mahabharata* is meant to be heard by all people, the rich and the poor, men and women alike. Book Six of the *Mahabharata* is the *Bhagavad-Gita*.

The Bhagavad-Gita

Considered the highlight of Smriti literature, the *Bhagavad-Gita* includes a famous dialogue between Krishna, an *avatar* who is an incarnation of Vishnu, the Hindu god who protects and preserves, and Arjuna, a warrior prince.

Krishna appears on earth at intervals to fight evil. In this story Krishna is Arjuna's good friend and charioteer. Krishna tries to convince Arjuna of the wisdom of doing battle against enemies, but Arjuna would rather show compassion.

As the warriors line up on the battlefield, he sees members of his own family on the enemy side. His dilemma is to choose for himself, for his family or for the gods. Arjuna argues that going to battle would destroy the family and hurt his cousins. Krishna argues that the warrior's role in society is to wage war, and fulfilling the role will help Arjuna have a better birth in the next life. Moreover, nobler than compassion, which is a disguise for Arjuna's grief, is to dispassionately perform his duty with faith and without desire for personal gain. Arjuna finally comes to see the wisdom of Krishna's argument and agrees to fight.

The Ramayana

The *Ramayana* is one of the most popular Hindu poems. Composed originally in Sanskrit, probably around 300 B.C.E., it tells the story of Prince Rama, one of the most loved deities in India.

The point of the story is that doing the right thing in accordance with the law, dharma, is often painful and self-sacrificial, but it is still the right thing to do.

SELECTED READINGS

Below are excerpts from *The Bhagavad-Gita*, and a summation of god-realization from *Bhagavad Mahapurana*.

THE BHAGAVAD-GITA

1. ARJUN'S DILEMMA

Arjun wants to inspect the army against whom he is about to fight

Seeing the Kauravs standing, and the war about to begin with the hurling of weapons, Arjun, whose banner bore the emblem of Lord Hanumaan, took up his bow and spoke these words to Lord Krishna: O Lord, please stop my chariot between the two armies until I behold those who stand here eager for the battle and with whom I must engage in this act of war. I wish to see those who are willing to serve and appease the evil-minded Kauravs by assembling here to fight the battle. Sanjay said: O King, Lord Krishna, as requested by Arjun, placed the best of all the chariots in the midst of the two armies facing Bhishm, Dron, and all other Kings, and said to Arjun: Behold these assembled Kauravs! There, Arjun saw his uncles, grandfathers, teachers, maternal uncles, brothers, sons, grand-sons, and comrades.

Arjun's dilemma

Seeing fathers-in-law, companions, and all his kinsmen standing in the ranks of the two armies, Arjun was overcome with great compassion and sorrowfully said: O Krishna, seeing my kinsmen standing with a desire to fight, my limbs fail and my mouth becomes dry. My body quivers and my hairs stand on end. The bow slips from my hand, and my skin intensely burns. My head turns, I am unable to stand steady, and O Krishna, I see bad omens. I see no use of killing my kinsmen in battle. I desire neither victory, nor pleasure nor kingdom, O Krishna.

What is the use of the kingdom, or enjoyment, or even life, O Krishna? Because all those—for whom we desire kingdom, enjoyments, and pleasures—are standing here for the battle, giving up their lives and wealth. I do not wish to kill teachers, uncles, sons, grandfathers, maternal uncles, fathers-in-law, grandsons, brothers-in-law, and other relatives who are about to kill us, even for the sovereignty of the three worlds, let alone for this earthly kingdom, O Krishna.

Arjun describes the evils of war

Eternal family traditions and codes of conduct are destroyed with the destruction of the family. Immorality prevails in the family due to the destruction of family traditions. And when immorality prevails, O Krishna, the women of the family become corrupted; when women are corrupted, many social problems arise. This brings the family and the slayers of the family to hell; because the spirits of their ancestors are degraded when deprived of ceremonial offerings of rice-ball and water. We have been told, O Krishna, that people whose family traditions are destroyed necessarily dwell in hell for a long time. Arjun sat down on the seat of the chariot with his mind overwhelmed with sorrow.

3. PATH OF KARMAYOG

The Supreme Lord said: In this world, O Arjun, a twofold path of spiritual discipline has been stated by Me in the past—the path of Self-knowledge (Jnana Yoga) for the contemplative, and the path of unselfish work (Seva, Karma Yoga) for the active. One does not attain freedom from the bondage of Karma by merely abstaining from work. Everyone is driven to action—helplessly indeed—by the forces of nature. The deluded ones, who restrain their organs of action but mentally dwell upon the sense enjoyment, are called hypocrites.

Why one should serve others?

One who controls the senses by a trained and purified mind and intellect, and engages the organs of action to selfless service, is superior, O Arjun. Therefore, O Arjun, becoming free from selfish attachment to the fruits of work, do your duty efficiently as a service to Me.

To help each other is the first commandment of the creator

Brahma, the creator, in the beginning created human beings together with selfless service (Seva, Yajn, sacrifice) and said: By Yajn you shall prosper, and Yajn shall fulfill all your desires. Nourish the celestial controllers (Devas) with selfless service (Seva, Yajn), and they will nourish you. Thus nourishing one another, you shall attain the Supreme goal. The celestial controllers (Devas), nourished by selfless service (Seva, Yajn), will give you the desired objects. One who enjoys the gift of Devas without offering them anything in return is, indeed, a thief. For a Self-realized person, who rejoices only with the Eternal Being (Brahma), who is delighted with the Eternal Being and who is content with the Eternal Being, there is no duty. (Such a person has no interest, whatsoever, in what is done or what is not done. A Self-realized person does not depend on anybody (except God) for anything.

Leaders should set an example

Therefore, always perform your duty efficiently and without any selfish attachment to the results, because by doing work without attachment one attains the Supreme Being. You should also perform your duty with a view to guide people, and for the universal welfare of society. O Arjun, there is nothing in the three worlds (heaven, earth, and the lower regions) that should be done by Me, nor there is anything unobtained that I should obtain, yet I engage in action. If I do not engage in action relentlessly, O Arjun, people would follow the same path in everyway. These worlds would perish if I do not work, and I would be the cause of confusion and destruction of all these people. As the ignorant work, O Arjun, with attachment to the fruits of work, so the wise should work without attachment, for the welfare of the society. The wise should not unsettle the minds of the ignorant, who are attached to the fruits of work, but should inspire others by performing all works efficiently without selfish attachment.

CORE BELIEFS

Hindus believe creation is cyclical. From the destruction of a previous universe Brahma arises to create a new universe; Vishnu sustains it through a cycle of birth, growth and decline; Shiva destroys the universe; and the cycle begins again.

Brahma

Brahma, the creator god, is also called Pitamaha, which means grandfather. Hindus regard Brahma as the ancestor of all the other gods and goddesses. He was born in a golden egg, and created the earth and every thing on it. Some later Hindu legends tell of Brahma's birth from a lotus flower that grew from the navel of Vishnu. Brahma is also the god who represents the priestly class of Hindus called Brahmans.

Brahma was the major god of Hinduism for about 1,000 years, but as Hinduism grew and changed, Brahma was not as central to Hindu worship as were Shiva, Vishnu and the Great Goddess. Today no part of

Hinduism worships only Brahma, but all temples dedicated to Shiva or Vishnu have images of Brahma in them. Brahma is often depicted as having four faces and four arms, and stands on a lotus flower throne.

Shiva

Shiva is both the destroyer god and the restorer. Shiva is represented by a *lingam*, an image of a penis. Shiva is a paradoxical god because he can symbolize both the virtues of abstinence and the sensual values of sexual union. He is a herdsman of souls and an avenger of wrongs.

Shiva has three eyes, two for outward vision and the third for inward vision. This third eye also has the ability to burn people with its gaze. He has a blue neck from swallowing poison. His hair is a coil of tangled locks, and he is the one who brought the sacred Hindu river, the Ganges, to earth by allowing it to flow through his hair.

Shiva has a partner goddess whose name is Kali (also known as Uma, Sati, Parvati, Durga, and Sakti). Shiva and Kali have two sons, Skanda and Ganesa.

Shiva is regarded by some Hindus as the Supreme Being and by others as forming a triad with Brahma and Vishnu. Shiva and his family live at the top of Mount Kailasa, one of the highest mountains in the Himalayas.

Vishnu

Vishnu is the protector and preserver of the universe. He is the lawgiver who establishes the dharma, the moral code, and the ritual practices of Hinduism. He is regarded by his worshipers as the supreme deity and savior and by others the preserver of the cosmos in a triad with Brahma and Shiva.

Vishnu is known and worshiped mainly through his manifestations of his nine earthly incarnations, or avatars, including that of Krishna, Rama and the historical Buddha. Hindus believe that his tenth avatar will herald the end of the world.

As Brahma faded from primacy, Vishnu rose. He appears when evil needs to be overcome and is the most popular Hindu god.

Vishnu also has female gods as his companions. They are Lakshmi, also called Sri, and Bhumidevi, symbolic of the earth. His home in the heavens is Vaikuntha.

Moksha

The main task of this world is to move beyond desires so that the soul can be released from the cycle of death and rebirth, called *samara*. Achieving release through Moksha can take lifetimes, and Hindus believe that the soul goes through many reincarnations. Birth is a sign that the person has not attained enlightenment or release.

Depending upon the Moksha, the consequence of action in this present life is that, at death, the soul, *atman*, is reborn in either a higher or a lower physical form. Through devotion or correct behavior, it is possible to ascend through the orders of reincarnation, achieve liberation from the cycle of rebirth and be reunited with the Divine Power.

Ahimsa or Non-Injury

Ahimsa is the foundation of nonviolence toward any living thing. However, the meaning is more complex than simply not trying to hurt something. It also means not doing injury, known or unknown, to any other thing.

The Sanctity of the Cow

Stemming from the importance of cows in the lives of early Indians, the cow represents divine and natural goodness, and should be protected.

The Caste System

In Hinduism human beings are divided into four classes determined by birth. A person's caste defines the job he or she may do, the marriage partner, how to dress, the religious practices the individual should adhere to, and the level of freedom to move about.

Impermanence of Life

According to Hinduism, nothing in life is permanent. By embracing yoga and other forms of prayer, people can choose between two paths in life—the path of desire and the path of renunciation. Those who seek the path of desire are bound to be unhappy, their victories fleeting. Those who choose the path of renunciation find happiness and eventually enlightenment.

Mantra

Meditation, according to Vedanta, is the repetition of a sacred formula—a *mantra*. Om is the first mantra in the *Vedas* and the *Upanishads*. Much of Mantra Yoga, as it is called, is done through *japa* (repetition, usually through a rosary). Mantras are chanted. Through their meaning, sound and chanting style, they help meditation focus for the *sadhaka* (practitioner). They can also be used to aid in expression of love for the deity, another facet of Bhakti Yoga akin to the understanding of the *murti*. They often give courage in exigent times and serve to help invoke one's inner spiritual strength. Indeed, Mahatma Gandhi's dying words are said to have been a two-word mantra to the Lord Rama: "*Hé Ram!*"

The most revered mantra in Hinduism is the famed Gayatri Mantra of the *Rig Veda* 3.62.10. Many Hindus to this day, in a tradition that has continued unbroken from ancient times, perform morning ablutions at the bank of a sacred river (especially the Ganges) while chanting Gayatri and Mahamrityunjaya Mantras.

Sanskrit is mostly used as a ceremonial language in Hindu religious rituals in the form of hymns and mantras.

BRANCHES OF HINDUISM

There are three divisions within Hinduism.

Specific Deity

This is more devotional than theological, and one's favorite deity tends to classify the school of thought and rituals. Vedism is devoted to the Veda gods; Brahmanism looks to Brahma; Vishnuism favors Vishnu; and Shivaism looks to Shiva. These are the four main deities, although each deity has thousands of branches.

Contemporary Hinduism would add two more.

Shaktism worships Shakti, the Divine Mother. Tantric Hinduism uses ritual sexual intercourse, accompanied by magic spells and divinations, to unite with the sexual power of the goddess Shakti.

Smartism accepts and worships all major forms of God—Ganesha, Siva, Sakti, Vishnu, Surya and Skanda. Following a meditative, philosophical path, Smartism is generally considered liberal and non-sectarian.

Chosen Way

The second division of Hinduism is based upon the chosen way to enlightenment. One may follow the Buddha's example and chose The Middle Way. Another might go his own way with Transcendental Meditation or Zen. There is the emotional Bhakti way. Some Hindus emphasize the use of mantras or *koans*. Some use yoga as their chosen way.

Guru

In Hinduism there are many gurus. Anyone who writes a commentary of the *Vedas* or the *Gita* becomes the head of a new denomination. There are now over 1,000 famous commentaries of the *Gita* alone. And only God knows how many not-so-famous ones!

HINDUISM IN THE MARKETPLACE

No centralized authority dictates Hindu business ethics.

Duties to family and caste are major influences. The actual caste system is complex, being composed of a vast array of sub-castes. The demand upon the Hindu is to accept his or her caste and all the obligations, privileges and limitations that are associated with it. Compounding the demands of caste is one's stage in life. The student is compelled to behave differently from an elderly person, just as the ethics of the priestly caste are not always the same as those of the warrior.

Gurus, wandering holy men, *sadhus* and sages teach ad hoc business ethics. Sacred scriptures give general moral guidance. They prohibit murder, theft, adultery and consuming alcohol. They promote kindness to others, respect for all life, vegetarianism and honoring elders.

Among general sanctions against immorality, *Anusana Parva* says, "One should not behave towards others in a way which is disagreeable to [them]. This is the essence of all morality. All other activities are due to selfish desire." *Taittiriya Upanishad* teaches that honesty is a key part of pure conduct: "Let your conduct be marked by truthfulness in word, deed, and thought." *The Law Code of Manu* gives the Hindu version of the golden rule. "Wound not others, do no one injury by thought or deed, utter no word to pain thy fellow creatures."

Hinduism promotes four goals in life: (1) love or pleasure that comes from karma, (2) gaining material wealth, (3) walking the path of dharma and (4) release from reincarnation. The second applies directly to the marketplace and, on occasion, might be stated in the Latin of another pantheistic culture: *Caveat Emptor.*

Dharma is supposed to mitigate, based as it is on sympathy, fairness, and restraint. Sin is to act selfishly instead of following dharma. Unfortunately, dharma depends upon which of the four castes you are born into, and into which of the four stages of life you are—student, householder, retiree or one who has renounced everything. The latter probably is not in the mood for any business. The other stages have different dharma, each set within the subjective context of the four goals in life, the ambiguities of which can confuse the Western businessperson.

It may be completely ethical from a Hindu businessperson's perspective to lie, cheat and steal if he believes that doing so promotes his goals in life. A Hindu acquaintance of mine summed up the problem this way:

"If you are suppose to be dishonest to achieve your dharma and do not do so, then you are not living a virtuous life. Your dharma says you are supposed to be a successful business owner. So, you do whatever it takes to achieve that. If being dishonest helps the business, the person is doing what is meant to be and that way can progress up the ladder of castes in each cycle of rebirth. If you are not supposed to be dishonest and you are simply greedy, you make up for that dishonesty by giving a donation to the temple. There is no incentive to be honest. These days you cannot trust anyone."

REFERENCES AND FURTHER READING

Capaldi, Nicholas. *Business and Religion: A Clash of Civilizations? (Conflicts and Trends in Business Ethics)*. Salem: M&M Scrivener Press, 2005.

Chu, Chin-Ning. *Thick Face, Black Heart: Thriving and Succeeding in Everyday Life and Work Using the Ancient Wisdom of the East*. Sydney: Allen & Unwin (Australia) Pty Ltd, 1995.

Dave, Nalini V. *Vedanta and Management: Relevance of Vedantic Concepts in Modern Management Practices*. New Delhi: Deep & Deep Publications, 1997.

Gupta, Dipankar. *Ethics Incorporated*. New Delhi: HarperCollins India, 2005.

Mckenzie, John. *Hindu Ethics: A Historical and Critical Essay, (The Religious Quest of India)*. Oxford: Oxford University Press, 1922.

Perrett, Roy W. *Hindu Ethics: A Philosophical Study (Monographs of the Society for Asian and Comparative Philosophy, 17)*. Honolulu: University of Hawaii Press, 1998.

Stackhouse, Max. *On Moral Business: Classical and Contemporary Resources for Ethics in Economic Life*. Grand Rapids: Wm. B. Eerdmans Publishing Company, 1995.

CHAPTER 6

SIKHISM

Treat others as thou wouldst be treated thyself.

Guru Angad

Macauliffe volume 2, page 29

Sikhism is the world's ninth largest religion with 23 million adherents. A Sikh is a practitioner of Sikhism. The word Sikh originates from the Punjabi language and means student or learner.

Over 60 percent of Sikhs live in the Northern Indian state of Punjab, forming about two-thirds of the population. Large communities of Sikhs live in the neighboring states of Haryana, Himachal Pradesh, Jammu and Kashmir, Rajasthan, Uttar Pradesh, Uttaranchal and Delhi. Because of Sikh migration in the late 19th Century C.E., there are now Sikh communities all over the world with significant numbers found in Canada, the United Kingdom, the Middle East, East Africa and Southeast Asia. More recently, immigrants have settled in the United States, Western Europe, Australia and New Zealand. Although Sikhs compose less than 2% of the Indian population, they are disproportionately represented in Indian politics, life and military.

Sikhism is a monotheistic religion that worships one, timeless, omnipresent, supreme creator called Akal Purakh. Sikhs teach a message of devotion and remembrance of God at all times, truthful living and social justice. Sikhs believe that the true path to achieving salvation and merging with God does not require renunciation of the world or celibacy. One must live the life of a householder, earning an honest living, and avoid worldly temptations and sins. Sikhism condemns superstitions, blind rituals, pilgrimages, and the worship of the dead and idols. Sikhism preaches that people of different races, religions and sexes are all equal in the eyes of God. Women may perform any Sikh ceremony. Sikhism is open to all through the teachings of its Ten Gurus, Sikh holy books and the teachings of *Sri Guru Granth Sahib*.

HISTORY

The strictly monotheistic faith of Sikhism developed in northern India in the midst of polytheistic religious culture during the 16th and 17th Centuries C.E. It was founded by Sri Guru Nanak Dev Ji, who lived between October 1469 and May 1539 C.E. in the village of Talwandi, now called Nankana Sahib, near Lahore in present-day Pakistan. Nanak was the first of the so-called Ten Gurus. He received a vision to preach the way to enlightenment and God. He believed in the fellowship of all humanity. Consequently he rejected both the Hindu caste system and idol worship.

His parents were Hindus and belonged to the merchant caste. Nanak was fascinated by religion even as a child. His desire to explore the mysteries of life eventually led him to leave home.

Nanak married Sulkhni of Batala, and they had two sons, Sri Chand and Lakhmi Das. Nanak's brother-in-law obtained a job for him in Sultanpur as the manager of a government granary.

One morning at the age of 28, Nanak made his daily trip to the river to bathe and meditate. Sikh legends say that this time he was gone for three days, and when he reappeared, he was filled with the spirit of God. He declared, "There is no Hindu and no Muslim," and then began his missionary work to proselytize this and other radical revelations.

He made four great journeys, traveling to all parts of India, and into Arabia and Persia, visiting Mecca and Baghdad. He spoke before Hindus, Jains, Buddhists, Parsees and Muslims. He spoke in temples and mosques, and at various pilgrimage sites. It was during this period that Nanak met Kabir (1441–1518), a saint revered by both Hindus and Muslims. It is very likely Guru Nanak also met Christian and Jewish missionaries during his extensive travels to the West. Christian missionaries were active in the southern parts of India visited by Guru Nanak.

Guru Nanak spoke out against rote religious rituals, pilgrimages, the caste system, the sacrifice of widows and the dependence on books to learn the true religion. Although he sought to combine the Hindu and Muslim faiths into a single religious creed, he never asked his listeners to follow him. He asked only that the Muslims to be true Muslims and the Hindus to be true Hindus.

After the last of these four great journeys, Guru Nanak settled in the town of Kartapur in Punjab on the banks of the Ravi. There he taught for another fifteen years. Followers from all over came to settle in Kartapur to learn, to sing hymns and to be with him. During this time his followers kept the religions in which they were born, but they became known as the Guru's disciples, or Sikhs.

Nanak told his followers that they could not live apart from the world because there should be no priests or hermits. During one of the common meals, a revolutionary principle of Sikhism began. It required the rich and poor, Hindu and Muslim, high caste and low caste, to sit together.

Before Guru Nanak died, he summoned his disciples and requested them to sing "Sohila," the evening hymn. He knew that his Hindu followers would want to cremate his body while his Muslim followers would try to bury it. To satisfy both factions, the funeral arrangements would require a miracle. When the sheet covering his corpse was lifted, all that remained were fresh flowers that were equally divided. The Hindus cremated their flowers and the Muslims buried theirs.

Because of its relatively young age and its tolerance of other religions, Sikhism is sometimes misunderstood to be merely a reform movement or branch of older existing religions. However, like all religions, there are some similarities as well as differences.

The most significant historical religious center for the Sikhs is Harmiandir Sahib (The Golden Temple) at Amritsar in the state of Punjab. It is the inspirational center of Sikhism but is not a mandatory place of pilgrimage or worship. All places where the book, *Sri Guru Granth Sahib*, is installed are considered equally holy for Sikhs.

The Ten Gurus

Sikhism was established and developed by the Ten Gurus during the period 1469 to 1708 C.E. The Ten are not considered divine but are thought of as enlightened teachers through whom God revealed his will. Starting with Sikhism's founder, each Guru appointed his successor.

(1) Guru Nanak Dev (1469–1539) founded Sikhism.

(2) Guru Angad Dev (1504–1552) developed Gurmukhi, the script used for the Punjab language, and composed 62 hymns that were later included in the *Guru Granth Sahib*.

(3) Guru Amar Das (1479–1574) became Guru at the age of 73 and organized three annual gatherings for Sikhs. He also set up the first pilgrimage site at Goindval Sahib and introduced Sikh rituals for birth and death. His most famous hymn, "Anand Sahib," is part of Sikh daily ritual.

(4) Guru Ram Das (1534–1581) founded Amritsar. His followers dug the pool that became the holy lake surrounding the Golden Temple. He composed the "Lavan Marriage Hymn" still used in Sikh marriages.

(5) Guru Arjan Dev (1563–1606) collected the hymns of previous Gurus and added 2,616 of his own to form the first sacred book of Sikhism. Guru Arjan started the compilation in 1601 and had a final draft in 1604. He called the book *Pothi Sahib* and, because he founded the Golden Temple, he installed the book there.

Pothi Sahib quickly became better known as *Adi Granth*. For the first time in history, the compiler of holy text would see its acceptance as sacred literature in his lifetime. A century after Guru Arjan died, his book would receive greater honor and a different name.

(6) Guru Hargobind (1595–1644) was the son of Guru Arjan. The son was said to be a military as well as spiritual leader, leading to conflict with the Mughal emperor, Shah Jahan.

(7) Guru Har Rai (1630–1661) was the grandson of Guru Hargobind.

(8) Guru Har Krishan (1656–1664) was the younger son of Guru Har Rai. A strain of nepotism starts to become apparent when one realize that Har Krishan was introduced to the high priesthood by his grandfather and was appointed Guru at the age of five. He died of smallpox three years later. He is the only Guru depicted in Sikh art without a beard.

(9) Guru Tegh Bahadur (1621–1675) was the Great-uncle of Guru Har Krishan and was barred from Amritsar by Sikh rivals. For that reason, he founded the Sikh center of Anandpur. Muslims beheaded him in Delhi for helping Brahmins avoid forcible conversion to Islam.

(10) Guru Gobind Singh (1666–1708) was the son of Guru Tegh Bahadur. Of the Ten, he is second only to Guru Nanak in importance. He is often shown prominently next to Nanak in Sikh artwork. He unsuccessfully resisted oppression by Mughal and Hindu rulers. He is remembered for demonstrating the Sikh ideal of the heroic saint-soldier. He founded the Khalsa and Sikh baptism, and composed many poems. His most lasting impact was to nominate the Sikh sacred book as the final and enduring "Guru."

After Guru Gobind's assassination, the Muslim Mughal rulers persecuted the Sikhs until 1799 when, under Ranjit Singh (1780–1839), they laid claim to a large part of northwest India. After Ranjit's death, the Sikh kingdom disintegrated into anarchy. The British moved into the Punjab, and the Sikh Wars followed, 1845–1849.

The Sikhs were defeated, and the British annexed Punjab. In the 20th Century the Sikhs were given control of their holy places. When the Indian subcontinent was partitioned in 1947, western Punjab became Pakistani territory and the eastern Punjab part of India. Because of civil unrest and persecution against the Sikhs in Pakistani Punjab, about 2,500,000 Sikhs moved into India.

SACRED TEXTS

The holiest of the Sikh scriptures is *Guru Granth Sahib*. It was compiled by Guru Arjan Dev, the fifth of the Ten Gurus, and became known as *Adi Granth*, which translates as "First Scripture."

In the first scripture are hymns from Guru Arjan and predecessors such as Guru Nanak, Guru Angad, Guru Amardas and Guru Ramdas. Further writings were taken from 15 renowned saints of both the Guru period and pre-Guru period, among them the works of Hindu, and the popular Muslim writers, Farid and Bhikhen.

Guru Gobind Singh added the hymns of Guru Tegh Bahadur in 1706 and two year later conferred on the book the title *Guru of the Sikhs*. The writings were then known as *Guru Granth Sahib*, which today's Sikhs usually shortened to just plain *Granth*.

Like much of the world scriptures, the text of the *Granth* deals mostly with one's relationship to God. The *Granth* is 1,430 pages long, divided into 39 chapters. It is composed of poetry and is arranged in musical measures. Thirty-one out of the 39 Chapters are headed by the musical measure, timing, rhythm and mood appropriate for signing the hymn that follows. There are 31 musical measures (*ragas*) used in the *Granth*.

Sikhs regard *Guru Granth Sahib* as the Living Guru and give it utmost respect. The *Granth* is always wrapped in clean sheets, ceremoniously opened every morning and deferentially closed at nighttime. It is placed on a small cot with cushions under it and on its sides. Sheets cover the *Granth* when it is open, and the open copy must be placed under a canopy. Every devotee must bow to it when the practitioner comes into its presence.

Seven other books complete the canon of Sikh holy literature: (1) *Dasam Granth*, (2) *Sarab Loh Granth*, (3) *The Hukam Namas*, (4) *Guru Hargobind*, (5) *Varan Bhai Gurdas I & II, Janam Sakhis* and (7) the works of Bhai Nand Lal.

SELECTED READINGS

For brevity, we will quote below only from *Guru Granth Sahib*.

ONE UNIVERSAL CREATOR GOD. THE NAME IS TRUTH.

CREATIVE BEING PERSONIFIED. NO FEAR. NO HATRED. IMAGE OF THE UNDYING, BEYOND BIRTH, SELF-EXISTENT.

BY GURU'S GRACE ~

CHANT AND MEDITATE:

TRUE IN THE PRIMAL BEGINNING. TRUE THROUGHOUT THE AGES.

TRUE HERE AND NOW. O NANAK, FOREVER AND EVER TRUE.

By thinking, He cannot be reduced to thought, even by thinking hundreds of thousands of times. By remaining silent, inner silence is not obtained, even by remaining lovingly absorbed deep within. The hunger of the hungry is not appeased, even by piling up loads of worldly goods. Hundreds of thousands of clever tricks, but not even one of them will go along with you in the end. So how can you become truthful? And how can the veil of illusion be torn away? O Nanak, it is written that you shall obey the Hukam of His Command, and walk in the Way of His Will. By His Command, bodies are created; His Command cannot be described. By His Command, souls come into being; by His Command, glory and greatness are obtained. By His Command, some are high and some are low; by His Written Command, pain and pleasure are obtained. Some, by His Command, are blessed and forgiven; others, by His Command, wander aimlessly forever. Everyone is subject to His Command; no one is beyond His Command. O Nanak, one who understands His Command, does not speak in ego. Some sing of His Power-who has that Power? Some sing of His Gifts, and know His Sign and Insignia. Some sing of His Glorious Virtues, Greatness and Beauty. Some sing of knowledge obtained of Him, through difficult philosophical studies. Some sing that He fashions the body, and then again reduces it to dust. Some sing that He takes life away, and then again restores it.

AAG MAAJH, CHAU-PADAS, FIRST HOUSE, FOURTH MEHL:

ONE UNIVERSAL CREATOR GOD. THE NAME IS TRUTH.

CREATIVE BEING PERSONIFIED. NO FEAR. NO HATRED.

IMAGE OF THE UNDYING, BEYOND BIRTH, SELF-EXISTENT.

BY GURU'S GRACE:

The Name of the Lord, Har, Har, is pleasing to my mind. By great good fortune, I meditate on the Lord's Name. The Perfect Guru has attained spiritual perfection in the Name of the Lord. How rare are those who follow the Guru's Teachings. I have loaded my pack with the provisions of the Name of the Lord, Har, Har. The Companion of my breath of life shall always be with me. The Perfect Guru has implanted the Lord's Name within me. I have the Imperishable Treasure of the Lord in my lap. The Lord, Har, Har, is my Best Friend; He is my Beloved Lord King. If only someone would come and introduce me to Him, the Rejuvenator of my breath of life. I cannot survive without seeing my Beloved. My eyes are welling up with tears. My Friend, the True Guru, has been my Best Friend since I was very young. I cannot survive without seeing Him, O my mother! O Dear Lord, please show Mercy to me, that I may meet the Guru. Servant Nanak gathers the Wealth of the Lord's Name in his lap.

MAAJH, FOURTH MEHL: The Lord is my mind, body and breath of life. I do not know any other than the Lord. If only I could have the good fortune to meet some friendly Saint; he might show me the Way to my Beloved Lord God. I have searched my mind and body, through and through. How can I meet my Darling Beloved, O my mother? Joining the Sat Sangat, the True Congregation, I ask about the Path to God. In that Congregation, the Lord God abides.

Read of the Lord's Glories and reflect upon the Lord's Glories. Listen continually to the Sermon of the Naam, the Name of the Lord, Har, Har. Joining the Sat Sangat, the True Congregation, and singing the Glorious Praises of the Lord, you shall cross over the treacherous and terrifying world-ocean. Come, friends, let us meet our Lord. Bring me a message from my Beloved. He alone is a friend, companion, beloved and brother of mine, who shows me the way to the Lord, the Lord of all. My illness is known only to the Lord and the Perfect Guru. I cannot continue living without chanting the Naam. So give me the medicine, the Mantra of the Perfect Guru. Through the Name of the Lord, Har, Har, I am saved.

MAAJH, FOURTH MEHL: I meditate on the Glorious Praises of the Lord of the Universe, and the Name of the Lord. Joining the Sangat, the Holy Congregation, the Name comes to dwell in the mind. The Lord God is our Lord and Master, Inaccessible and Unfathomable. I am forever a sacrifice, to my Friend and Intimate Divine Guru. || Pause ||

When I could not be with You for just one moment, the Dark Age of Kali Yuga dawned for me.

ONE UNIVERSAL CREATOR GOD. TRUTH IS THE NAME.

CREATIVE BEING PERSONIFIED. NO FEAR. NO HATRED.

IMAGE OF THE UNDYING. BEYOND BIRTH. SELF-EXISTENT. BY GURU'S GRACE:

SHALOK SEHSKRITEE, FIRST MEHL:

Who is the mother, and who is the father? Who is the son, and what is the pleasure of marriage? Who is the brother, friend, companion and relative? Who is emotionally attached to the family? Who is restlessly attached to beauty? It leaves, as soon as we see it. Only the meditative remembrance of God remains with us.

O Nanak, it brings the blessings of the Saints, the sons of the Imperishable Lord. Cursed is loving attachment to one's mother and father; cursed is loving attachment to one's siblings and relatives. Cursed is attachment to the joys of family life with one's spouse and children. Cursed is attachment to household affairs. Only loving attachment to the Saadh Sangat, the Company of the Holy, is True. Nanak dwells there in peace. The body is false; its power is temporary. It grows old; its love for Maya increases greatly. The human is only a temporary guest in the home of the body, but he has high hopes. The Righteous Judge of dharma is relentless; he counts each and every breath. The human body, so difficult to obtain, has fallen into the deep dark pit of emotional attachment. O Nanak, its only support is God, the Essence of Reality. O God, Lord of the World, Lord of the Universe, Master of the Universe, please be kind to me.

CORE BELIEFS

Sikhism believes in (1) a single all-powerful God; (2) the utterances and teachings of the Ten Gurus, from Guru Nanak to Guru Gobind Singh; (3) the sacred authority of "The Living Guru," *Guru Granth Sahib,*

(4) living an honest life and treating all equally; and (5) allegiance to no other religions.

All religions have temples where people can gather together to contemplate God and pray. Where Sikhs gather is called a *Gurdwara*, which means "Gateway to the Guru."

In Sikhism, one's personal dedication to living a good life and meditating on God are important, but equally important is corporate participation in the *Sangat* (congregation). There are thousands of Gurdwaras throughout Punjab and the rest of the world, serving as community centers for adherents. There are no restrictions on who may enter a Gurdwara for prayer. People of all religions are welcome.

A feature common to all Gurdwaras around the world is the *Langer*, the free community kitchen. Food is served communally to all peoples regardless of race, creed, color, caste, sex, age or national origin. This is the tangible and living symbol of Sikhism's spirited belief in true unity.

Many of the Gurdwaras in Punjab have a pool (*sarovar*) in which to bathe. In Sikhism one can wash in these pools as one wishes, but the person should be pure inside to get any real benefit. The underlying thought is: though the water may cleanse you on the outside, it cannot clean you on the inside. A pure heart is what smells sweet to God.

Unlike some religions, pilgrimage is not a part of Sikhism. Sikhs may visit any Gurdwara, considering them all equally sacred, although The Golden Temple is regarded as the most important of the Sikh shrines.

BRANCHES OF SIKHISM

There are three divisions within Sikhism. The first two are Udasis and Sahajdharis. Udasis are an order of ascetics and holy men who often serve as missionaries. Sahajdharis are clean-shaven and do not follow the *Khalsa* tradition.

The Khalsa take their name from "Pure," the title Guru Gobind Singh bestowed on all Sikhs who have been baptized in a 300-year-old ceremony called Amrit Sanchar. The Khalsa must carry five symbols, *Panj Kakka*, also know as the "Five Ks." These are:

Kesh

Uncut hair is meant to represent the natural appearance of saint-hood. Some argue that saints are not distinguished by hair length, but you can spot the Khalsa who thinks it is important. Khalsa wear a small turban underneath a bigger turban. In that way the kesh, or uncut hair, is kept in place.

Kanga

A small comb is the second saintly symbol that gains increasing practical use with each passing year.

Kacha

Short trousers help a warrior when he is moving about the battle-field. They also remind him of the need for chastity.

Kara

This iron bangle is a sign of restraint and bondage, and is symbolic of dedication to the Guru. Guru Gobind Singh proclaimed that wearing the Kara would remove the fears of all practitioners.

Kirpan

The sword for defense symbolizes dignity, power and courage, all of which will be needed if the sword has to be drawn.

The Khalsa began when Guru Gobind Singh asked a crowd of Sikhs which ones would die for their faith and for them to step into a tent. One man walked into the tent, and the Guru followed. A few seconds later only the Guru emerged, holding his sword covered in blood. After asking if there were any more volunteers, four people went into the tent, ready to be slaughtered for their faith.

It was then that the crowd found out that none of the five men were actually killed. They were the first of The Khalsa Brotherhood. They were baptized, and in turn baptized others who follow the Five Ks and the other requirements into "the brotherhood."

SIKHISM IN THE MARKETPLACE

Sikh beliefs translate into three practices in commerce.

The first is that honest labor and hard work (*Kirat Karna*) are the approved way of life. It is considered honorable to earn one's daily bread and not beg or use dishonest means. It is written that, "He who eats what he earns through his earnest labor and from his hand gives something in charity; he alone, O Nanak, knows the true way of life."

The Sikh work ethic is legendary and translates into greater economic prosperity than apparent with their peers in other faiths. The state of Punjab is known as India's breadbasket, owing to its significant production of staple crops, and supports one of the most industrialized economies in the nation. In India and across the world Sikhs are either an important mercantile class or successful in the skilled professions. These accomplishments are owed to a close-knit community structure, progressive farming techniques and a cultural emphasis on education.

While belief in hard work bodes well for individual Sikhs and their communities, at times it opens the door to corruption, nepotism and cronyism. This is particularly true when they deal with non-Sikhs. Priority is placed on community first and foremost, and the interests of outsiders are hardly noted by comparison.

The second practice is harmony. Sikhs believe that the purpose of life is to love God. They use self-discipline to replace greed, desire, anger and pride with contentment, humility and forgiveness. *Guru Granth Sahib* says "Do not cause any being to suffer, and you shall go to your true home with honor."

Sikhs emphasize the importance of work with hands, head and heart in the service of themselves, their families and their social communities.

In following God's will, Sikhs hope to lose their sense of self-importance and gain a sense of harmony with God.

While Sikh theology emphasized equality and unity from the time of Guru's Nanak's explicit condemnation of the caste system, socio-economic divisions have developed among Punjabis of the urban mercantile class. There have arisen caste-like divisions with other Punjabi communities. This re-emergence of the caste-like system facilitates corruption in trade because one group favors its own kind at the expense of other groups.

Lastly, to Sikhs, cheating, lying, black-marketeering, profiteering and bribery are not approved by the Father of the Universe. God's displeasure cannot bring peace and happiness, but too often it does not end bad behavior. *Gaurhi Sukhmani Mahla Panjvaan* instructs that "Unethical action may bring more money and give satisfaction at least temporarily."

To cheat someone is strongly disapproved in the Sikh Scriptures: "To deprive someone of his or her due share is like eating pork for a Muslim and eating beef for a Hindu. The Guru will stand by you if you do not consume someone else's share, which is deadly for you."

A problem arises when Sikh teachings run headlong into the laws of governments. The Mormon pioneers in America might have identified. Those who wanted to establish polygamy in Utah Territory viewed the Federal Government with absolute disdain. Washington, DC did not comport with what their Prophet and martyr Joseph Smith, Jr. had said about multiple wives.

Similarly, Sikhs may believe that amoral governments make laws for people who do not know what ethics mean. What Guru is a bureaucrat following, if any? How true to Islam, Hinduism or Christianity are parliamentarians? Aren't a judge's "ethics" just a cover for hypocrisy? And aren't the government's sanctions against people of true understanding just stepping-stones of greed?

"They," whoever they are, are absent in the description of the highest transaction of Sikh business: "The greatest business that will give you good name in the Court of God is your truthful dealing with absolute Truth—God."

That is Truth with a capital T. No mention of a laborer's name, the Fire Marshall or the competitor across the mountains because the secular world (or those ignorant of religious matters) need not apply to the absolute. Hence, when Sikh tradition finds itself in conflict with minimum wage regulations, income tax laws, health and safety codes, it's Truth with a capital T versus law with a lower case l. Guess which scores more knockouts.

REFERENCES AND FURTHER READING

Ajitsingh, Charanjit. *The Wisdom of Sikhism*. Oxford: Oneworld Publications, 2001.

Cole, Owen. *Teach Yourself Sikhism*. New York: McGraw-Hill, 2005.

Duggal, Kartar. *Philosophy and Faith of Sikhism*. Honesdale: Himalayan Institute Press, 1988.

Nesbitt, Eleanor. *Sikhism: a Very Short Introduction*. New York: Oxford University Press, USA, 2005.

Rama, Swami. *Japji*. Honesdale: Himalayan International Institute of Yoga Science and Philosophy of the U.S.A, 1987.

Singh, Nikky-Guninder. *The Name of My Beloved*. San Francisco: Harper San Francisco, 1995.

Singh, Pashaura, and N. Barrier. *Sikhism and History*. Oxford: Oxford University Press, 2004.

PART FOUR

⊙

RELIGIONS ORIGINATING IN THE MIDDLE EAST

CHAPTER 7

CHRISTIANITY

And as ye would that men should do to you,

do ye also to them likewise.

Luke 6:31

Christianity is the world's largest religion with 2.1 billion practitioners. It originates from the ancient patriarch Abraham whose faith in God was the wellspring of Judaism. Islam also calls Abraham the father of its faithful. Besides a common origin for the world's three major monotheistic religions, each focuses on sin as the world's most pressing problem, and each offers a path from sin to salvation.

Unlike the other two, Christianity demands no human effort to take at least the first steps along the path of salvation. Those steps come from what is called grace, a free gift from God. God desires people to be saved from the consequences of their sin and, according to Christian doctrine, takes those consequences upon himself. Then he expects people to strive toward holiness so that they may have complete fellowship with him.

Christians do not think that individuals can understand God except as he reveals himself to them. Even with God initiating the relationship, he is an all-powerful, all knowing, eternal presence who must deal with what is very finite and limited and willfully rebellious. The rebellion began with what Christians call Original Sin.

Original Sin is represented by the biblical story of Adam and Eve, the progenitors of the human race. They were created as free moral agents, and God did not interfere with their free choice to break his single warning to them: do not try to be as gods. From their act of rebellion, all people throughout all ages have inherited the propensity for wrongdoing. Because we are corrupted, we cannot approach the incorruptible unless he makes the first move.

God's first and continuing move is the revelation of himself as creator of the natural world and as lawgiver of the processes that keep the universe ticking. More father-like, he historically showed his plan and purpose for creation to the prophets of Israel, and he charged the children of Israel to take their knowledge of him to be "a light unto the Gentiles." But it is in a radically different form he finally showed himself in ways that most people most everywhere might best understand. It was if he were saying, "Now! Now do you see? This is what I am like!"

He became a man.

Because no human can do anything about his or her sins except to become more enmeshed in them (and more distant from God), the mercy of God is embodied in the birth, death and resurrection of Jesus Christ. Jesus was the perfect human representation of God's love and forgiveness. As such, Jesus was the only worthy sacrifice whose death could pay for the cost of sin for all people. Once Jesus had died for the sins of humanity, he was raised from the dead and became united again with the Father in heaven, yet still distinct as the Second Person of the Trinity.

The Trinity is a single God composed of three distinct persons— God the Father, God the Son and God the Holy Spirit. That a triune God can still be one is like a woman simultaneously being a beloved child, a faithful wife and a devoted mother.

Obviously, God is more complex than any maleness attributed to him; and the Trinity, only a limited explanation of all his attributes. Yet for Christians, it as the Father and in the male-like persons of the Trinity that God chooses to show some of the vast majesty and mystery of himself. These revelations suggest the familial relationship God hopes humankind will have with him.

The faithful who trust in Jesus for the grace of salvation take his promise literally that the Holy Spirit dwells within them and that, together with the Spirit, they will be with Jesus and the Father in heaven after they die. What exactly that looks like or means has bankrupted the vocabulary of theologians from the earliest Christian times to the present. This is the one reason that makes Jesus, "fully God yet fully human," so immediate and approachable.

HISTORY

Over its 2,000-year history Christianity spread from ancient Palestine to Europe, the Americas, and large parts of Africa and Oceania. It is growing rapidly in the Middle East and Asia, particularly in Korea and China. Although difficult to calculate because of persecution by the Communist government, Chinese Christians probably represent the greatest increase in converts in recent years.

Christianity is based upon the claims of Jesus of Nazareth, a Jew who lived his 1st Century C.E. life in the Roman province of Palestine in the Middle East. Indirectly at first and then with increasing boldness, Jesus said that he was God incarnate, the long awaited Messiah. The Hebraic word for Messiah suggests a priestly "King of kings," not necessarily supernatural, but one who will bring justice to all the earth. Supernatural or not, this implies quite a bit of power and presumably would make ordinary leaders, both secular and religious, redundant. The implications hounded Jesus until his execution at the age of 33.

During his three-year public ministry, Jesus performed numerous miracles, claiming they were part and parcel of the Kingdom of Heaven. He alleged that he had the authority to perform miracles because he was the Son of his Father in heaven. More importantly, he had the power to forgive sin. Indeed, Jesus claimed for himself the sacred name of God, a blasphemous crime under Hebraic law. Because the Jewish religious authorities were subservient to Rome, they had to turn Jesus over to Governor Pontius Pilate for punishment. Pilate did not recognize the blasphemy but ordered the prisoner crucified on the grounds that Jesus could perhaps lead a revolt against Caesar.

Following Jesus' death upon a cross and burial in a tomb, witnesses said that he rose from the dead and was taken with glory into heaven. As this gospel (literally "good news") spread from Palestine into the wider Roman world, Jesus was increasingly referred to as Christ, Christ being the Greek title for Messiah. A Christian originally meant "little Christ," a term used derisively at first, but by 313 C.E., it had gained full honor when the Emperor Constantine elevated Christianity to the state religion of the Roman Empire.

Christians believe that Jesus was born at the time of the census of Caesar Augustus and that his birth is the dividing point of history. Because of the pervasive influence of Christianity in the West, calendar dates were delineated as either B.C. (Before Christ) or A.D. (Latin for Anno Domini, meaning "After God"). Elsewhere, the success of Christianity's material offspring—capitalism, scientific rationalism and technological innovation in warfare—caused non-Christian cultures to utilize the same dating system at least in international affairs. The more recent usages of B.C.E. (Before the Current Era) and C.E. (Current Era) are secular attempts to diminish Christianity's influence and be more inclusive of other religions, but they are anchored to the same historical points in time.

Secular criticism of Christianity's role in Western history and in the colonization of the Third World presents a laundry list of crimes—the Inquisition, witchcraft trials, forced conversion of indigenous peoples, disdain for pagan cultures, pogroms against Jews, enslavement of blacks and so on. The specific charges are very often true. However just as often, the numbers of victims are exaggerated; the guilt of singular nations or ethnic groups is expanded to include all of Christendom; and what happened centuries ago gets telescoped as if to appear it was regular practice only yesterday.

More scholarly secularists do not disagree with other claims made for Christianity—the creation of capitalism and the university system, the transformation of magic into science, the overturn or downsizing of monarchy, tolerance of other religions, the abolition of slavery, the emancipation of women, legislation to end the exploitation of child labor and the ironic notion that you can have non-religious governance of devoutly religious people.

The belief in Jesus' resurrection from the dead, coupled with Jesus' promise to take his followers with him to Heaven, has motivated Christians to try to do good throughout the centuries. It also has sustained them in the face of persecution that still goes on from Southeast Asia to Saudi Arabia, and has taken a brutal turn in the Sudan where mass slaughter, enslavement and rape are common.

SACRED TEXTS

Christians can read of the life of Jesus, as well as his predecessors, in the only Christian holy book, the Bible. It consists first of the Old Testament, the longer part, sections of which are considered sacred to Judaism and Islam. Christians have started referring to the Old Testament as the Hebrew Bible. By any name, it chronicles the lives of Jews and others who lived before Jesus and to whom God had promised a savior.

The second, shorter part of the Christian Bible is called the New Testament. Unique to Christianity, it centers around the figure of Jesus and his effect on the world. Christians believe that Jesus is the savior foretold in the Old Testament, so instead of looking for a savior, they await the return, or Second Coming, of Jesus.

The New Testament is comprised of the Four Gospels, gospel meaning "good news." The good news records the ministry of Jesus and his promises of salvation. History of the early church follows with *Acts of the Apostles*. The Epistles are letters to some of the early churches, but in large part are meant to be instructive to all churches for all time. The New Testament closes with the *Book of Revelation*, which is filled with metaphors about the end of time.

Bibles used by Roman Catholics include apocryphal books. They are not considered sacred but are regarded as literature that has didactic purpose and explains the origins of some doctrines. Most Protestants, while accepting their literary value, think it is unnecessary, if not subversive to faith, to include the Apocrypha in the Bible.

The Four Gospels

(1) *The Gospel of Matthew*, according to Christian tradition, was authored by a hated tax collector named Levi. At the time of his writing, however, he had become Mathew, one of the Twelve Apostles proclaiming the love of Christ. His target audience was Jewish-Christian communities in predominantly Jewish areas.

Matthew portrays Jesus as the new Moses—the lawgiver who led the Jews from slavery in Egypt to the Promised Land. From sin, you might say, to salvation. Mathew includes the Beatitudes that resemble the Ten Commandments in their guidelines as to how to live. They call Christians to work on humility, peacefulness and prayerfulness, and ask them to willingly fast, mourn and undergo persecution.

(2) *The Gospel of Mark* is tantalizingly vague about the background of its author. Mark is not mentioned in the list of the disciples, but according to an early church tradition, Mark followed Peter and copied down Peter's words.

Some suggest that Mark wrote to a Latin community, gearing the text to Gentiles who struggled with the idea of following Jesus because he was a Jew. The majority of Jews at that time were meticulous of their exclusivity and regarded Gentiles on the level of dogs.

(3) *The Gospel of Luke* was written by a physician who never met Jesus but who is widely recognized as a good historian who meticulously gleaned information from others.

Luke portrays Jesus as prayerful teacher and as someone devoted to the salvation of all people. Luke's gospel is particularly partial to women. Of all the gospels, *Luke* most completely portrays Jesus as a master in the use of parables; that is, stories about ordinary things that evoke deeper spiritual meanings.

(4) *The Gospel of John* was written by one of the first of Jesus' disciples, probably the youngest and the one to whom Jesus was most endeared. Jesus charged John to take care of his mother after the crucifixion.

John is more poetic and symbolic than the other gospel writers, and he immediately paints a portrait of Jesus as pre-existent and divine. John describes Jesus as "the bread of life," "the light of the world," "the good shepherd," and, "...the way, the truth and the life." For John, disciples are called to believe in Jesus with their entire minds, hearts and souls.

The Acts of the Apostles

This book details the history of the beginnings of Christianity after Jesus' death and resurrection. It was written by Luke as the second part of a long letter to a friend. Naturally, Luke did not expect his letter to be divided into a gospel and *Acts*. Like all New Testament writers, he could not foretell that anything he wrote would be made part of a holy book.

The first part of *Acts* is about the Apostles in Jerusalem. Then the focus switches to a persecutor of Christians, a zealous, scholarly Jew named Saul. He receives a miraculous encounter with God, converts with the same zeal that he persecuted and becomes known as Paul, Apostle to the Gentiles.

Epistles

Twenty-one letters are attributed to Peter, Paul, James, John, Jude and others. These writings address specific spiritual and social problems in the early Christian community.

The Book of Revelation

This blood and thunder account is about the end of time. Authorship is attributed to John when he was very old and in exile. He was encouraging the Christian community that was undergoing a new and seemingly relentless wave of persecution. The book is filled with symbolism, dream sequences and visions. They are meant to remind believers that their suffering will end soon and that a new life with God will bring peace for all eternity.

Apocrypha

The word apocrypha means hidden. Many biblical scholars suggest that the apocryphal was withdrawn from mainstream use because the text is too mysterious or contains esoteric lore that can't be backed up.

In addition to the Hebrew apocryphal books, Christian apocryphal books have been discovered. These present information about the beliefs and practices found in the various movements of early Christianity.

The Christian church never accepted any of these apocryphal books as canonical. However, it is interesting to note that 2 *Maccabees* contains the seeds of exclusively Catholic teachings such as the Doctrine of Purgatory and Masses for the Dead.

Historically, the important thing about the Apocrypha is that these books give insight into the religious climate that prevailed for roughly 300 years. This time period was between the last writing in the Hebrew

Bible, about 250 B.C.E., and the beginning of New Testament writings at about 50 C.E. The Apocrypha describes political upheaval, war, hostile occupation, religious conflict and a falling away from faith. The strong implication is that the world was on its last legs, and a great battle between good and evil would soon occur.

SELECTED READINGS

The Gospel of John

John 3

There was a man of the Pharisees, named Nicodemus, a ruler of the Jews: The same came to Jesus by night, and said unto him, "Rabbi, we know that thou art a teacher come from God: for no man can do these miracles that thou doest, except God be with him."

Jesus answered and said unto him, "Verily, verily, I say unto thee, except a man be born again, he cannot see the kingdom of God."

Nicodemus saith unto him, "How can a man be born when he is old? Can he enter the second time into his mother's womb, and be born?"

Jesus answered, "Verily, verily, I say unto thee, except a man be born of water and [of] the Spirit, he cannot enter into the kingdom of God. That which is born of the flesh is flesh; and that which is born of the Spirit is spirit. Marvel not that I said unto thee, Ye must be born again. The wind bloweth where it listeth, and thou hearest the sound thereof, but canst not tell whence it cometh, and whither it goeth: so is every one that is born of the Spirit."

Nicodemus answered and said unto him, "How can these things be?"

Jesus answered and said unto him, "Art thou a master of Israel, and knowest not these things? Verily, verily, I say unto thee, We speak that we do know, and testify that we have seen; and ye receive not our witness. If I have told you earthly things, and ye believe not, how shall ye believe, if I tell you of heavenly things? And no man hath ascended up to heaven, but he that came down from heaven, even the Son of man which is in heaven. And as Moses lifted up the serpent in the wilderness, even so must the Son of man be lifted up: That whosoever believeth in him should not perish, but have eternal life.

"For God so loved the world, that he gave his only begotten Son, that whosoever believeth in him should not perish, but have everlasting life. For God sent not his Son into the world to condemn the world; but that the world through him might be saved. He that believeth on him is not condemned: but he that believeth not is condemned already, because he hath not believed in the name of the only begotten Son of God."

First Epistle to the Corinthians

1 Corinthians 13

Though I speak with the tongues of men and of angels, and have not charity, I am become as sounding brass, or a tinkling cymbal. And though I have the gift of prophecy, and understand all mysteries, and all knowledge; and though I have all faith, so that I could remove mountains, and have not charity, I am nothing. And though I bestow all my goods to feed the poor, and though I give my body to be burned, and have not charity, it profiteth me nothing.

Charity suffereth long, and is kind; charity envieth not; charity vaunteth not itself, is not puffed up. Doth not behave itself unseemly, seeketh not her own, is not easily provoked, thinketh no evil; Rejoiceth not in iniquity, but rejoiceth in the truth; Beareth all things, believeth all things, hopeth all things, endureth all things.

Charity never faileth: but whether there be prophecies, they shall fail; whether there be tongues, they shall cease; whether there be knowledge, it shall vanish away. For we know in part, and we prophesy in part. But when that which is perfect is come, then that which is in part shall be done away. When I was a child, I spake as a child, I understood as a child, I thought as a child: but when I became a man, I put away childish things. For now we see through a glass, darkly; but then face-to-face: now I know in part; but then shall I know even as also I am known.

And now abideth faith, hope, charity, these three; but the greatest of these is charity.

CORE BELIEFS

Christianity adopted from Judaism the concept of a single, eternal God who created the universe from nothing and invented time at the point of creation. Christianity expanded the understanding of God with unique beliefs about the divinity of Christ and the nature of God as a Holy Trinity.

Christians believe in the literal resurrection of Jesus Christ. He is not a mere spirit but retains a bodily form that is no longer subject to either decay or to the laws of the natural world. He can be in many places at once, and in one of his post-death appearances to his earliest disciples, he barbecued fish and ate with them.

The anniversary of the resurrection is the most important date on the Christian calendar. It took place during the Jewish Passover. The day of Christian celebration, Easter, started as a pagan holiday that Christians subjugated for their own use.

Jesus' miraculous birth to a virgin is celebrated at Christmas with hymns, special services and the giving of gifts. Most Protestant Christians did not regard Christmas as a special day until the end of the 19th Century. At that time manufacturers and merchants saw the potential of commercializing the holiday. Their success is apparent to almost any observer.

The purpose of life for Christians is to do the will of God in this world and, by Jesus' death on the cross, be worthy of a heavenly life with him in the next. Christians understand that one of the commandments for this world is "The Great Commission," the marching order for evangelism. Christians are to go out into the entire world, baptize non-believers in the name of the Trinity and train them to be disciples of Christ. At the very least, they are supposed pray for those actually going out and doing the discipling and, if they can, provide financial support.

New Christians are baptized by being either sprinkled with water or total immersion. Symbolically, the water cleanses them from sin and drowns them as sinful people. Coming out of the water ritualizes the resurrection of a transformed life. Depending on the branch of Christianity, people are baptized either as babies or when they reach an age of moral awareness and consent. A phrase often heard, "Born again," is not the result of baptism but rather a description of a person who has declared Jesus Christ as their personal Lord and Savior.

Christianity teaches that the most intimate connection God can make with his people is to suffer along with them. Although Christians are urged to pray for healing and for relief from tribulation, the knowledge that God is with them during difficult times comforts those who believe that personal suffering can produce positive outcomes. Trusting in God no matter what the circumstances is difficult, but Christians accept this as essential if they are to mature in faith.

In Christianity time is linear, although there are two different understandings of where it is headed. One suggests that, as believers become more and more Christ-like, they will be able to pacify and renew the world, bringing about the Kingdom of God on earth. The second views the world as so full of suffering and wrongdoing that an antichrist will rise to rule. Then Christ will have to return and defeat the antichrist in a great battle that inaugurates a reign of peace. In the minds of many Christians these views are not mutually exclusive.

Christianity views itself as the fulfillment of Judaism, whereas Judaism views Christianity as a heretical cult. Jewish converts to Christianity sometimes call themselves Fulfilled Jews or Messianic Jews, terms particularly irksome to friends and family still awaiting a Messiah. Strange, but nonetheless heartening to beleaguered Jews in Israel, is how most Evangelical American Christians have sided with them in almost every issue due to the scriptural promise of God's favor on nations and individuals who bless the Jews.

In some Muslim and Hindu countries it is a crime to practice Christianity and a capital offense to convert. Nonetheless, many Muslims regard Jesus as a prophet, and many Hindus accept him as a sage. Those terms rankle informed Christians because of Jesus' claims to be God. They argue that a mere prophet or teacher who says he is God has to be mentally ill or lying through his teeth. He cannot be a good man worthy of respectful but lesser titles.

Jesus' claims to be the only way to salvation and eternal life imply an exclusivity to Christianity that angers anyone who would rather tolerate many paths to salvation. Oddly, this anger is most apparent among theologians and preachers who call themselves Christians yet question the historical existence of Jesus. They take biblical accounts of Jesus and his miracles as myth invented by followers to bamboozle the unwary. Practicing Christians wonder why these skeptics bother to include themselves as fellow believers.

Apostles' Creed

The basic beliefs of Christianity are summed up in what is called the Apostles' Creed. It has received this title because of its great antiquity, dating from within a half-century or so from the last writings of the New Testament. With very little variation it is recited in unison by Christians of all stripes. Some do it every Sunday, others much less often.

I believe in God, the Father Almighty,

maker of heaven and earth,

and in Jesus Christ, His only begotten Son, our Lord:

Who was conceived of the Holy Spirit,

born of the Virgin Mary,

suffered under Pontius Pilate,

was crucified, died and buried.

He descended into hell.

The third day He arose again from the dead.

He ascended into heaven

and sits at the right hand of God the Father Almighty,

whence He shall come to judge the living and the dead.

I believe in the Holy Spirit, the holy catholic church,

the communion of saints,

the forgiveness of sins,

the resurrection of the body,

and life everlasting.

Amen.

BRANCHES OF CHRISTIANITY

As time progressed, Christianity divided into three major branches. Today there is a diversity of doctrine and practice among numerous groups that label themselves Christian. These groups are sometimes called denominations, although for various theological reasons some reject the classification. However, widely divergence groups can be described in terms of common traditions brought about by historical similarities and differences.

Roman Catholicism

The Roman Catholic branch is the successor to the church established in Rome soon after Christ's death. Its spiritual genealogy begins with the earliest disciples of Jesus. The Pope, the spiritual leader of the Roman Catholic Church, traces the lineage of his office back to St. Peter.

Currently, the Roman Catholic Church composes the largest branch of Christianity. In it are included so-called Latin Rite churches and several Eastern Catholic communities that have closer affinity with what became known as Orthodoxy. Together, their baptized members total about one billion.

Eastern Christianity

During the 4th Century the governance of the Roman Empire became distinct from that of the Byzantine Empire. Mirroring the distinction between East and West, the churches in Europe displayed some doctrinal differences from those in Asia Minor. In 1054 C.E., for mostly political reasons, the Roman Catholic Church broke from the church headquartered in Constantinople, now Istanbul, Turkey. Eastern Orthodoxy was officially born.

Orthodox churches are largely national, each associated with a particular country. Orthodoxy is common in Russia, Greece, Romania, Bulgaria, the Ukraine and Armenia. Baptized parishioners in these countries and in enclaves abroad number about 300 million.

Protestantism

Deeply rooted issues of dogma and practice caused a further split in the West. The Protestant branch of Christianity denounced the Roman Catholic Church and the authority of the Pope during the Reformation of the 16th and 17th Centuries. The results were at times very bloody, as suggested by the Hundred Years War. Ironically, what started as Catholics and Protestants killing each other ended with more important secular divisions, giving rise to armies of Catholics and Protestants fighting the mixed armies of political and national rivals.

Initially, the Protestant movement became popular in Scandinavia, England and the Netherlands. It swept North America, starting with the successful settlement of English colonists.

Protestantism eventually divided into many denominations that arose in response to further disputes over doctrine and practice. Some of the denominations today are Anglican, Baptist, Anabaptist, Lutheran, Methodist, Presbyterian and Pentecostal. Members of each sometimes distinguish themselves as unified on cross-denominational issues, e.g., charismatic, evangelical and reformed. A growing trend in the Protestantism is the rise of non-denominational churches with no centralizing beliefs or organization.

The worldwide total of Protestants ranges from 592 to 650 million.

CHRISTIANITY IN THE MARKETPLACE

Christian business ethics can be summed up as, "Love thy neighbor as thyself," and have become the *de facto* standard in international business today, even in countries where native religions don't encourage business ethics.

The Bible is the bedrock on which all Christian conduct is supposed to rest. In Paul's letter to the Romans, he teaches, "Recompense to no man evil for evil. Provide things honest in the sight of all men." He expounds on honesty in a letter to the Ephesians: "Wherefore putting away lying, speak every man truth with his neighbor."

Christians nurture patience and diligence through their expectations that Jesus will return and finish the work of the Messiah. *Hebrews* 6 sums the result in an admonishment not be lazy: "And we desire that each one of you may show the same diligence unto the fullness of hope even to the end: that ye be not sluggish, but imitators of them who through faith and patience inherit the promises."

Christians view the Bible as containing the moral duties for the whole human race. God expected Adam and Eve to work both before and after the fall. *Psalm 104* places human work in the cycle of nature:

"When the sun rises... Man goes forth to his work and to his labor until the evening."

Other parts of the Bible likewise treat work as a duty and industriousness as a virtue. Paul enjoined Christians to, "...be ready for any honest work." To the Thessalonians Paul commanded, "We exhort you... to work with your hands." In the Old Testament, Nehemiah recalled that the wall of Jerusalem was rebuilt with dispatch because, "...the people had a mind to work."

Industriousness is one of the chief traits of the virtuous wife described in *Proverbs* 31. "She does not eat the bread of idleness," but instead, "works with willing hands...and rises while it is yet night." *Proverbs* suggests many rewards for diligence in labor, among them, "He who tends a fig tree will eat its fruit."

Conversely, the Bible condemns laziness or sloppiness in work. In *Ecclesiastes* we read, "Through sloth the roof sinks in, and through indolence the house leaks." To the Thessalonians, Paul disparaged those who lived, "...in idleness, mere busybodies, not doing any work."

Again to the Thessalonians, Paul uses his work ethic as a model for others to follow: "For you yourselves know how you ought to imitate us; we were not idle when we were with you, we did not eat anyone's bread without paying, but with toil and labor we worked night and day, that we might not burden any of you. It was not because we have not that right, but to give you in our conduct an example to imitate."

But as we have seen with other religions, Christians often separate faith from business dealings. The rationale for the dichotomy is twofold.

First, there are many degrees of belief among Christian. Some are culturally Christian, wearing only the label, while others are zealous in their faith. The nominal Christian borrows ethics from the world, not the church.

Second, one of the theological tenants of Christianity is grace from God for forgiveness of sins. Therefore a number of practitioners erroneously believe that they can commit premeditated sin in the marketplace (or anywhere else for that matter) and expect God to forgive them without their having to genuinely repent and change their ways.

Such behavior, though, is inherently un-Christian because it ignores the twin doctrines of creation and sovereignty. The apostle Paul states in *Colossians* that no realm of life is beyond the lordship of Jesus. Indeed, all things were created, "...through him, in him and for him." Christ's authority sustains the created order, extending over, "...thrones, or dominions, or principalities, or powers." This accords Jesus Christ power over all beings and institutions. No human activity, including the practice of business, falls outside of his lordship. To argue otherwise is heresy.

Christian ethics cannot be relegated to part-time status, applied only on evenings and weekends. On the contrary, Martin Luther correctly asserted that Christian vocation is best expressed in life's most common experiences.

REFERENCES AND FURTHER READING

Bertch, David P. *Biblical Business Ethics: Exploring Secular Ethical Values and Alternative Christian Approaches (Minding Your Own Business Series: Book 2)*. Fort Worth: Good Works Press, 1994.

Burkett, Larry. *Business By the Book: Complete Guide of Biblical Principles for the Workplace*. Nashville: Nelson Business, 2006.

Dawn, Marva J. *Keeping the Sabbath Wholly: Ceasing, Resting, Embracing, Feasting*. Grand Rapids: Wm. B. Eerdmans Publishing Company, 1989.

Julian, Larry S. *God Is My CEO: Following God's Principles in a Bottom-Line World*. Cincinnati: Adams Media Corporation, 2002.

Marsden, George M. *The Soul of the American University: From Protestant Establishment to Established Nonbelief*. New York: Oxford University Press USA, 1996.

Smith, Gordon T. *Courage & Calling: Embracing Your God-Given Potential*. Dowers Grove: InterVarsity Press, 1999.

Williams, Oliver F. *Full value: Cases in Christian Business Ethics (Experience and reflection)*. New York: Harper & Row, 1978.

CHAPTER 8
ISLAM

That which you want for yourself,

seek for mankind.

Sukhanan-i-Muhammad, 63

With 1.3 billion people claiming to worship Allah, Islam is the world's second largest religion. Before Islam came along, first Judaism then Christianity claimed Abraham as patriarch of their faiths. Abraham had two children—the younger Isaac, whom Jews and Christians denote "the son of promise"—and the older Ishmael, a serving girl's illegitimate son whom Muslims deny was illegitimate and allege deserved all the rights and blessings God bestows on the firstborn.

Muslims assert that the main written record of God's revelation to humanity is the Qur'an. It includes God's direct words to the Prophet Muhammad and to earlier prophets such as Adam, Noah, Abraham, Moses and Jesus. Muslims argue that parts of the Christian Gospels, Jewish Torah and Jewish prophetic books have been forgotten, misinterpreted, incorrectly edited or purposefully distorted. With that perspective, Muslims view the Qur'an as the flawless and immutable correction of Jewish and Christian scriptures, and its author as the last and most exalted of prophets. Mohammad's teachings will last until *Qiyamah*, The Day of the Resurrection.

Many people believe that Islam has a similar idea of God as Judaism and Christianity—that God is a single creator, revealer and redeemer of the world. Christian and Jewish critics counter that the God of both the Hebrew and Christian Bibles believe that God encourages freedom, love, forgiveness, and prosperity and the Muslim God does not do so. Even Muslims in the Middle East would contend that there is a large gap separating them from militant Islamists regarding the nature of God.

Regardless, Muslims call God Allah, abbreviating the Arabic term *al-ilea*, which means "the God" and is the same kind of word theologically that Jews and Christians use to describe their God, Yahweh, in Hebrew. Muslim visual images of Allah are forbidden because artistic depictions may lead to idolatry. Most Muslims believe that God is incorporeal, making any two or three-dimensional depictions impossible anyway. Muslims describe God by the many divine attributes mentioned in the Qur'an.

There is no official authority that decides whether a person is accepted into—or dismissed from—a community of believers known as the *Ummah*. There is one formality of acceptance, the recitation of the *Shahada*, the statement of belief in Islam that should be said with sincerity of heart, with the intention of behaving in a manner befitting the community of Islam.

The *shari'ah*, Arabic for "well-trodden path," is Islamic law as elaborated by traditional Islamic scholarship. The Qur'an is the foremost source of Islamic jurisprudence.

The second source is the *Sunnah of Muhammad* and the early Muslim community. The Sunnah is not itself a text like the Qur'an, but is extracted by analysis of the recorded oral traditions (*hadith*, meaning report in Arabic). The Sunnah contains narrations of Muhammad's sayings, deeds and actions.

Ijma, the consensus of the community of Muslims, and *qiyas*, analogical reasoning, are the third and fourth sources of shari'ah.

Islamic law covers all aspects of life, from the broad topics of governance and foreign relations all the way down to issues of daily living. Islamic laws covered expressly in the Qur'an are referred to as *hudud* laws and include the five crimes of theft, highway robbery, intoxication, adultery and falsely accusing another of adultery, each of which has a prescribed *hadd* or punishment that cannot be mitigated.

The Qur'an also details laws of inheritance, marriage, restitution for injuries and murder, as well as rules for fasting, charity and prayer. However, the prescriptions and prohibitions may be broad and varied in their applications. Islamic scholars, the *ulema*, have elaborated systems of law based on these broad rules, supplemented by the hadith reports of how Muhammad and his companions interpreted them.

Not all Muslims understand the Qur'an in its original Arabic. Thus when Muslims are divided in how to handle situations, they seek the assistance of a *mufti*, an Islamic judge, who can advise them based on Islamic shari'ah and hadith.

Along with Judaism and Christianity, Islam sees humanity's sin as the world's main problem and offers a path to salvation from sin. The Islamic way is to prove surrender to the will of Allah as taught by his prophet Muhammad. If this is done before the Last Day of Judgment, believers cross the bridge that leads to the gardens of paradise.

HISTORY

In Arabic, Islam means literally "to surrender; to obey." The history of that obedience centers on a single person, namely Mohammad, who was born outside Mecca around 570 C.E. He was raised by an uncle, entered the caravan trade and married a wealthy widow. His prosperous life included ownership of slaves, marriage to a second widow when the first died and the taking of a third wife when she was 14 years old.

Round about Mohammad were Bedouins, some nomadic, some settled agriculturalists. They were broken into clans and tribes that were bound by Arabic dialects, a boundless capacity to remember feuds, and webs of sometimes-contradictory alliances. The majority followed polytheistic religions. Mohammad was familiar with these and with what was taught by religious minorities—Jews, Christians and Zoroastrians.

At the age of 40, while mediating in a cave, Mohammad began to receive messages from Allah. They were accompanied by convolutions, and initially Mohammad was afraid that he was demon possessed. His wife, others and finally Mohammad himself believed that his symptoms were due to the powerful presence of the Angel Gabriel. At first Mohammad conveyed what he was receiving only to kinfolk, but what he taught about strict monotheism spread rapidly to non-related followers. Visitations and revelations continued until Mohammad's death at the age of 63. They were compiled for future generations in the Qur'an.

The most divisive message from Allah was that Mohammad was God's last and truest prophet, topping a line that extended from Abraham and Moses to Jesus. That didn't play well in Mohammad's hometown. He and his followers were persecuted and forced to move from Mecca. The *hijra* ("the flight" in English) marks the first date of the Islamic calendar.

Mohammad and company took refuge under the Christian King of Ethiopia. For a time, like his host, Mohammad looked to Jerusalem as his spiritual home. Then he was called to Medina to settle a dispute. He did so by absorbing the factions into his own religious community, made Medina its headquarters and from there launched an eight-year war to subdue Mecca. The direction of a Muslims in prayer changed during the war from bowing toward Jerusalem to bowing toward Mecca.

Jews and Christians, whom Mohammad called "people of the book," rejected him as their prophet just as the citizens of Mecca originally had. This hurt him deeply. Mohammad initially preached tolerance, switched to a policy of uneasy co-existence in which Islam had to be in charge and eventually saw a glorious end of the world heralded by the Muslim slaughter of all Jews.

Mohammad's conquest of Mecca led to extending his ideas to neighboring cities and tribes, but before he died, he had not appointed a successor, and that would extend faction-fighting even farther. Some followers championed one of the original converts; others wanted a member of a powerful political family; still others insisted that the leader should come from Mohammad's own family.

From the debate came the Sunni, the Shi'a and the Sufis. Sunni are "followers of the prophet's way" and don't think a blood descendant of the prophet necessarily knows the way. The Sunni today make up the largest branch of Islam. The Shi'a believe that leadership should be based on heredity. The Sufis contend that orthodox Islam is too mechanical, and Sufi mystics seek direct personal experiences with Allah.

After the Prophet came leaders who were unifiers by either blood or persuasion. Just as Arabic Muslims were settling down to enjoy their expanding empire, Mongols invaded from the East. For nearly a century, the Mongols ruled from India to the Sinai Desert, but the Mongols quickly adopted the religion of the conquered Arabs. Thus successions of Asian, Aryan and other ethnic groups took Islam with them as they took down the Byzantine Empire and eventually spread to the Pacific.

Constantinople, the overrun eastern capitol of Orthodox Christianity, became the center of the Turkish dominated Ottoman Empire. From the middle of the 15th Century C.E. to the 17th Century, the Ottomans dominated much of the Arab world and many lands in Eastern Europe.

Simultaneously, Christian countries in Western Europe were generally expanding and colonizing, and specifically mounting crusades to wrest Muslims from the Holy Land, Spain and the Balkans.

The Ottoman Empire was in steep decline at the outbreak of World War I, and made the bad bet of choosing the cause of Germany and the Austro-Hungarian Empire. Arabs joined the Allies only to be betrayed when the victorious Allies carved up Arabic lands into French and English colonies, and promised Jews a homeland in Palestine.

World War II saw the literal Nazification of Arab leaders. After distancing themselves from the defeated Third Reich, these Arab leaders formed nationalist movements for self-determination. Revolutionary bloodshed and rhetoric overcame the exhausted reticence of European nations to give up their colonies. Independent nations were created that commingled warring branches of Islam and feuding ethnic groups.

SACRED TEXTS

Muslims believe that the prophet Muhammad received the Qur'an in bits and pieces over a period of 23 years. The Qur'an is approximately the same length as the New Testament, provides the guidelines for living a life that is pleasing to Allah and thus prepares the believer for the Day of Judgment. As the perfect earthly representation of God's words, the Qur'an cannot be adequately translated and so should be read or (preferably) heard in Arabic.

By the time it was complete, the Qur'an contained 114 *suras*, or chapter-length books. The suras are not arranged in the order in which Muhammad received them. With the exception of the first sura, *The Opening*, the others are arranged from longest to shortest. This arrangement is believed to be deliberate and divinely directed.

Each sura contains verses, or *ayat*, meaning signs. Each sura deals with a particular topic, revealed through the sura's title. All but one sura, the ninth, begins with the words "In the name of Allah, the Most Beneficent, the Most Merciful..." called the *Bismillah*.

The opening of the first sura, called the *al-Fatiha*, typifies Islam. It is used in daily prayers and at many religious moments.

SELECTED READINGS

The First Sura of the Qur'an

In the name of Allah, the Most Beneficent, the Most Merciful.

Praise be to Allah, the Lord of the Worlds, the Beneficent, the Merciful,

Master of the Day of Requital.

Thee do we serve, and Thee do we beseech for help.

Guide us on the right path, The path of those upon whom Thou hast bestowed favors, Not those upon whom Though hast bestowed favors, Not upon whom wrath is brought down no those who go astray.

From the Fourth Sura of the Qur'an

An-Nisa (Women)

....And whoever disobeys Allah and His Messenger and goes beyond His limits, He will cause him to enter fire to abide in it, and he shall have an abasing chastisement.

If any of your women are guilty of lewdness, Take the evidence of four (Reliable) witnesses from amongst you against them; and if they testify, confine them to houses until death do claim them, or Allah ordain for them some (other) way. As for those of your women who are guilty of lewdness, call to witness four of you against them. And if they testify (to the truth of the allegation) then confine them to the houses until death take them or (until) Allah appoint for them a way (through new legislation). And as for those who are guilty of an indecency from among your women, call to witnesses against them four (witnesses) from among you; then if they bear witness confine them to the houses until death takes them away or Allah opens some way for them.

If two men among you are guilty of lewdness, punish them both. If they repent and amend, leave them alone; for Allah is Oft-returning, Most Merciful. And as for the two of you who are guilty thereof, punish them both. And if they repent and improve, then let them be. Lo! Allah is ever relenting, Merciful....

....Men are the protectors and maintainers of women, because Allah has given the one more (strength) than the other, and because they support them from their means. Therefore, the righteous women are devoutly obedient, and guard in (the husband's) absence what Allah would have them guard. As to those women on whose part ye fear disloyalty and ill conduct, admonish them (first), (Next), refuse to share their beds, (And last) beat them (lightly); but if they return to obedience, seek not against them Means (of annoyance): For Allah is Most High, great (above you all).

Men are in charge of women, because Allah hath made the one of them to excel the other, and because they spend of their property (for the support of women). So good women are the obedient, guarding in secret that which Allah hath guarded. As for those from whom ye fear rebellion, admonish them and banish them to beds apart, and scourge them. Then if they obey you, seek not a way against them. Lo! Allah is ever High, Exalted, Great.

From the Eighth Sura of the Qur'an

Al-Anfal (Spoils of War)

And fight them on until there is no more tumult or oppression, and there prevail justice and faith in Allah altogether and everywhere; but if they cease, verily Allah doth see all that they do. And fight them until persecution is no more, and religion is all for Allah. But if they cease, then lo! Allah is Seer of what they do. And fight with them until there is no more persecution and religion should be only for Allah; but if they desist, then surely Allah sees what they do.

From the Forty-seventh Sura of the Qur'an

Muhammad

....those who believe and work deeds of righteousness, and believe in the (Revelation) sent down to Muhammad - for it is the Truth from their Lord, - He will remove from them their ills and improve their condition. And those who believe and do good works and believe in that which is revealed unto Muhammad - and it is the truth from their Lord - He riddeth them of their ill-deeds and improveth their state. And (as for) those who believe and do good, and believe in what has been revealed to Muhammad, and it is the very truth from their Lord, He will remove their evil from them and improve their condition.

This because those who reject Allah follow vanities, while those who believe follow the Truth from their Lord: Thus does Allah set forth for men their lessons by similitudes...

....Therefore, when ye meet the Unbelievers (in fight), smite at their necks; At length, when ye have thoroughly subdued them, bind a bond firmly (on them): thereafter (is the time for) either generosity or ransom: Until the war lays down its burdens. Thus (are ye commanded): but if it had been Allah's Will, He could certainly have exacted retribution from them (Himself); but (He lets you fight) in order to test you, some with others. But those who are slain in the Way of Allah, - He will never let their deeds be lost

Now when ye meet in battle those who disbelieve, then it is smiting of the necks until, when ye have routed them, then making fast of bonds; and afterward either grace or ransom till the war lay down its burdens. That (is the ordinance). And if Allah willed He could have punished them (without you) but (thus it is ordained) that He may try some of you by means of others. And those who are slain in the way of Allah, He rendereth not their actions vain. So when you meet in battle those who disbelieve, then smite the necks until when you have overcome them, then make (them) prisoners, and afterwards either set them free as a favor or let them ransom (themselves) until the war terminates. That (shall be so); and if Allah had pleased He would certainly have exacted what is due from them, but that He may try some of you by means of others; and (as for) those who are slain in the way of Allah, He will by no means allow their deeds to perish.

CORE BELIEFS

Muslims believe that there is but one God, Allah, who has spoken to humanity through many prophets, of whom Muhammad is the most important. Allah is the supreme lawgiver, and his laws are for the whole of creation, not just for human beings.

Although Muslims believe that Allah is absolutely one and indivisible, they have 99 names for him. Each name represents an aspect of Allah and includes appellations such as the Merciful One, the Wise, the Seer, the Witness, the Protector, the Benefactor, the Creator, the Judge, the Rewarder, the Forgiver, etc. These many names express the idea that God cannot be contained by one simple name, word or thought.

In addition to the Qur'an, Muslims look to hadith, the sayings and deeds attributed to the prophet Muhammad, and find explicit instructions regarding how to live in a way that is pleasing to God. Every Muslim is directly responsible to God for acting in accordance with these rules and creating a "good" society as defined by Allah and the Qur'an.

Muslim identity is inextricably linked to the social and political order. Islam is not only a guide for each believer but also a guide for the societies they build.

The core beliefs, or requirements, of Islam are contained in the Five Pillars of Islam:

(1) The First Pillar. Shahada, the Muslim profession of faith, is to be said on waking and before going to sleep: *I witness that there is no god but Allah, and that Muhammad is the prophet of Allah.*

(2) The Second Pillar. *Salat* is the rather precise prayer ritual to be performed 5 times a day by all Muslims over the age of 10. Prayers may be recited individually but preferably communally. They are said on hands and knees with heads bowed: (a) between first light and sunrise, (b) after the sun has passed the middle of the sky, (c) between mid-afternoon and sunset, (d) between sunset and the last light of the day, and (e) between darkness and dawn.

(3) The Third Pillar. *Sawm* is the abstaining from food each day during Ramadan, the ninth Muslim month. From dawn to sunset the adherent also fasts from bodily pleasures.

(4) The Fourth Pillar. *Zakat* is giving alms to the poor. The minimum should be 2.5 % of one's savings each year.

(5) The Fifth Pillar. *Hajj* is the pilgrimage to Mecca that all physically able Muslims should make at least once in their lives. Mecca is the most holy place for Muslims

The Concept of Creation

The story of creation is based on the belief that Allah brought the world and everything in it into existence with the simple command, "Be!" As Allah's creation, the universe shows perfect design and order, and all things are possessed by—and come from—Allah.

Humanity

Human beings are the most important of Allah's creations. According to Qur'anic law, all individuals are born inherently good. Islam does not have a doctrine of Original Sin as does Christianity and Judaism. The closest thing that comes to Original Sin is humanity's tendency towards arrogance that leads people to forget their place in Allah's world and to commit acts that are contrary to the spirit of Islam.

To remind people of their proper place, Muslims must surrender to the code, the Five Pillars of Islam. The concept of struggling to become everything that Allah would want in a human being is termed *jihad*. Jihad is also the word used for a holy war that justifies killing apostates and non-Muslims.

The Day of Judgment

The Qur'an portrays life as a "fleeting gift." For this reason, people must adhere to the Islamic code of existence or face the wrath of Allah at the time of reckoning. When they die, souls are judged whether they should be sent to the heavens or to the hells as described in the Qur'an.

Each soul, accountable for the use of time on earth, must stand alone, without the benefit of intercession or excuse, and be judged by Allah.

BRANCHES OF ISLAM

Each Islamic religious denomination has significant theological and legal differences from the others, but they possess essentially identical beliefs. The major branches are Sunni and Shi'a. Sufism is considered as a mystical inflection of Islam and, although considered a separate branch, will not be described here.

Sunni

The Sunnis make up about 85% of present day Muslims. According to Sunni believers, when Muhammad died, he did not designate a successor. The community chose a successor, called a caliph, who became the political leader of the community.

Sunni Muslims also believe that the community must follow the examples of the Sunnah, the ethical and religious code derived from the sayings and deeds of Muhammad. In the Sunni branch, the religious and political authority in Islam rests with the community, guided by Islamic law, and a consensus about the Qur'an by Islamic scholars and political leaders.

Shi'ite

The Shi'ites believe that Muhammad designated his cousin and son-in-law Ali to be the religious leader of Islam.

For Shi'ites all authority is vested with the imams or mullahs and, ultimately, the ayatollah. The charisma and authority of these leaders guides the teachings of Islam.

A sect within Shi'ites, the Twelver Shi'as, believes that The Twelfth Imam is soon to come. He will be known as Muhammad ibn Hasan ibn Ali. More importantly, he will be the *Mahdi* or the ultimate savior of humanity. The Twelver Shi'as believe that they can usher in the Mahdi's ascension by causing the end of the world. Other Shi'ite sects, as well as Sunnis, do not agree with the Twelver Shi'as' chronology for the Twelfth Imam and have diverse opinion about who the Mahdi is and what he will do.

The Muslim faith is becoming an increasingly volatile catalyst in today's international scene. As Islam grows and spreads throughout the world, Muslim extremists have sought to shift the balance of power in many regions, and have seized power in parts of Africa and Asia.

Muslim populations in Russia and the European Union continue to grow rapidly. Russia's Muslim population has increased by 40 percent since 1989, to about 25 million. Experts say that if current trends continue, nearly one third of Russia's population will be Muslim by mid-century.

Growing ethnic tensions in Russia have begun to mirror those of its European neighbors. There are between 9 and 15 million Muslims living throughout Europe today, and Islam has become the largest religious minority. Considering current population trends, it is likely that the number of Muslims in Europe will continue to grow exponentially.

The major terrorist group aligned with Sunni Muslims is Al-Qaeda. Hezbollah, which is generally considered the most effective terrorist organization in the word, is composed of Shi'ite Muslims. There is debate whether these and other groups can set aside sectarian differences and fully unite against the West.

ISLAM IN THE MARKETPLACE

Like most religions, the Qur'an teaches honesty, patience and charity. Like most followers of other religions, Muslims practice these virtues inconsistently, particularly when dealing with non-believers.

In Chapter 16 of the Qur'an, honesty and honoring promises made in Allah's name is important to, "...fulfill the covenant of God once you have pledge it, and do not break any oaths once they have been sworn to. You have set up God as a Guarantee for yourself; God knows everything you are doing."

Chapter 40 teaches patience and trust in Allah: "So be patient; surely the promise of Allah is true." The hadith reinforces long-suffering with a quote from Abu Da'ud (817–889 C.E.), one of the six chief compilers of Islamic tradition: "Muslims who live in the midst of society and bear with patience the afflictions that come to them are better than those who shun society and cannot bear any wrong done to them."

Islam' s version of the Golden Rule, "Not one of you is a believer until he desires for his brother what he desires for himself," is found in 40 *Hadith of an-Nawawi* 13.

Charity, particularly giving alms to the poor, is central in Islam as represented by its inclusion in the Five Pillars of Islam. An economically self-sufficient Muslim is expected to give alms in an act called zakat in Arabic. Giving to charity shows that one's faith is Allah is true and that the individual is not controlled by material possessions. The prophet Muhammad often cited charity as a central virtue of Islam as recalled by the Hadith of Bukhari: "A man once asked the Prophet what the best thing was in Islam, and he replied, 'It is to feed the hungry and to give the greeting of peace both to those one knows and to those one does not know.'"

The standard used for determining what is right or wrong in business is guided by the shari'ah and the collection of previous *fiqh* judgments. The latter include (1) Islamic legal interpretations; (2) organizational factors; and (3) individual quirks such as stages of moral development, personal values and personality, family influences, peer influences, life experiences and other situational factors.

The bottom line is that what is ethical for me under Islamic law may not be ethical for you, and what was unethical today, maybe ethical tomorrow. This creates an ambiguity about what is the appropriate moral conduct.

REFERENCES AND FURTHER READING

Beekun, Rafik Issa. *Islamic Business Ethics (Human Development Series)*. Herndon: International Institute of Islamic Thought, 1997.

Chapra, M. Umer. *Islam and Economic Development: A Strategy for Development with Justice and Stability (Islamization of Knowledge)*. Herndon: International Institute of Islamic Thought and Islamic Research Institute, 1993.

Denny, Frederick Mathewson. *Introduction to Islam, An (3rd Edition)*. Upper Saddle River: Prentice Hall, 2005.

El-Diwany, Tarek. *The Problem with Interest*. London: Kreatoc Ltd., 2003.

Iqbal, Munawar. *Distributive Justice and Need Fulfillment in an Islamic Economy (Islamic Economics Series)*. Leicestershire: The Islamic Foundation, 1988.

Kamali, Mohammad Hashim. *Islamic Commercial Law: An Analysis of Futures and Options*. Cambridge: Islamic Texts Society, 2000.

Siddiqi, Muhammad Nejatullah. *Banking Without Interest*. Ann Arbor: New Era Publications, 1983.

CHAPTER 9

JUDAISM

What is hateful to thee, do not to another.

That is the whole law and all else is explanation.

The Talmud, *Shabbat* 31a

Judaism is the world's fourteenth largest religion with 14 million people who call themselves Jews. It is the oldest of the three Abrahamic faiths that include Christianity and Islam.

Normally, religions are defined by adherents having shared beliefs about God or a deity and/or race. Judaism is unique in that, to be a Jew, you do not have to believe anything that Judaism teaches. The only requirement is that you have to be born of a Jewish mother.

Religious Jews primarily believe that their performance in this life will change and save the adherent from eternal damnation, and simultaneously change and save the world. In simplistic terms, one's good deeds are weighed in a balance against one's bad deeds. Nonetheless, God is filled with loving kindness and is eager to forgive transgressions as long as the believer is heartily repentant of bad behavior. Unlike the Christian who believes that even repentance is impossible without intervention or grace from God, the Jew takes the responsibility upon himself.

In Judaism, God is completely different from the world and from human beings. Therefore God could not become a person such as Jesus. Moreover, the Jesus of the New Testament died on a cross and thus did not meet the Jewish criteria for being the warrior Messiah who defeats evil.

Christians argue that there are two messianic "sons" presented in Scripture. The first is "a man of sorrows acquainted with grief," upon whom the Father would lay the sins of the world. The second comports with Judaism in that the world still awaits a messianic king who will crush evil with an iron rod.

Terms used primarily in the United States—Judeo-Christianity and Judeo-Christian ethics or morality—recognize widespread agreement on the ethical teachings of the two religions. In spite of deep division about the meaning of messianic passages in the Hebrew Bible, devout believers in both camps are in large agreement about the rest of the Old Testament.

"Devout" is the key word in the preceding paragraph. As indicated, one may be a non-practicing Jew or a secular Jew but, because of one's mother, still be as Jewish as an Hasidic rabbi with forelocks.

By contrast, modern Christians sometimes demonstrate that they harbor neither religious feelings nor beliefs, that they are as secular as atheists and sometimes less ethical. However, they are taught in Sunday Schools that faith, not bloodline, is a primary requirement for considering oneself a believer.

HISTORY

The Hebrew Bible is an account of the Israelites' relationship with God as reflected in their history from the beginning of time until the building of the Second Temple (around 350 B.C.E.). This relationship is often portrayed as contentious with Hebrews struggling between their faith in God and their attraction to other gods. Individual struggles with belief also abound, first and most directly, with Jacob, whose original name meant "usurper" because he tricked his older brother out of his birthright. Later, Jacob became known as Israel, the father of the Twelve Tribes of Israel and thereby all Israelites.

"Hebrew" pre-existed the term "Israelite." According to Orthodox Judaism and most religious Jews, the biblical patriarch Abraham was the first Hebrew. *Genesis* records that he was the first since Noah to publicly reject idolatry and preach monotheism. As a result, God promised Abraham would have children: "Look now toward heaven and count the stars, so shall be your progeny."

Abraham's first child was Ishmael and his second son was Isaac, whom God said would continue Abraham's work and inherit the Land of Israel (then called Canaan).

God sent the patriarch Jacob and his children to Egypt where, after many generations, they became enslaved, a state of servitude that lasted 400 years. Then God sent Moses to lead the Israelites' exodus from Egyptian bondage. Forced to wander for a generation in the desert before entering the promised land of Israel, the Israelites supposedly shook off the habits of slavery. Early in this school of hard knocks, God led the Israelites to Mount Sinai where he gave Moses "The Ten Commandments" and them the Torah.

God designated the descendants of Aaron, Moses' brother, to be a priestly class within the Israelite community. They first officiated in the tabernacle, a portable house of worship, and later were in charge of worship in the Temple in Jerusalem.

Once the Israelites had settled in the land of Israel, the tabernacle was planted in the city of Shiloh for over 300 years, during which time God provided great men, and occasionally women, to rally the nation against attacking enemies, some of which were sent by God as a punishment for the sins of the people. This is described in the *Book of Joshua* and the *Book of Judges*. As time went on, the spiritual level of the nation declined to the point that God allowed the Philistines to capture the tabernacle in Shiloh.

The people of Israel then told Samuel the prophet that they wanted to be governed by a permanent king, as were other peoples. Samuel grudgingly acceded and appointed Saul, a great but prideful man, to be their king. When the people pressured Saul into going against a command conveyed to him by the Lord, God told Samuel to appoint David in his stead.

From humble origins as a shepherd boy to an outlaw hunted by the jealous Saul, David proved his bravery and cunning, finally becoming not only a great king but also, after his death, an archetype of a warrior Messiah. The biblical account of his reign doesn't pull punches about David's flaws. He was a murderer as well as an adulterer, but as the Bible puts it, he had "a heart after God," was willing to admit wrongdoing, accept the consequences and seek mercy.

Once King David was established, he told the prophet Nathan that he wanted to build a permanent temple to honor God, who had bestowed so much upon David and his nation. Because David had been involved in many wars, it was judged inappropriate for him to build an edifice representing peace, but God promised that his son Solomon would be allowed to fulfill David's desire.

Solomon did construct a permanent temple in Jerusalem, but after his death the permanence of the domain was split asunder. Two kingdoms emerged, Israel to the north, and Judah and its capital Jerusalem to the south. Rampant idolatry followed for several hundred years until

God allowed Assyria to conquer Israel and exile its people. The southern Kingdom of Judah for a while remained under the rule of the House of David; however, as in the north, idolatry increased to the point that God allowed Babylonia to conquer the kingdom, destroy the Temple that had stood for 410 years and exile many of the people to Babylonia. These events are described the *Book of Isaiah* and the *Book of Jeremiah,* along with the promise that those in exile would be returned after seventy years.

After seventy years the exiles were allowed back into Judea under the leadership of Ezra, and the temple was rebuilt. The Second Temple stood for 420 years before it was destroyed by the Roman general (later emperor) Titus. The temple is to remain in ruins until a descendant of David arises to restore the glory of Israel.

From 587 B.C.E. until 1948 C.E. such glory as remained was in the shadows of larger, dominating empires—Babylonian, Persian, Greek, Roman, Byzantine, Islamic, Christian, Turkish and British.

After the forced exile by the Romans in what is known as the Diaspora, the majority of Jews migrated to Europe and North Africa, but they continually prayed to return to Israel where there always remained a remnant. Prayers became a reality in the first half of the 20th Century C.E. when the Zionist Movement inspired and financed waves of immigration from Europe and neighboring Arab countries to Palestine.

At that time Palestine referred to an area of land controlled first by the Turks before World War I and then the British afterwards. The occupants of Palestine were either Arab, Jewish or conquerors. The term Palestinian originally referred to Jordanian refugees after the Six Day War of 1967.

The extermination of six million European Jews by Nazi Germany touched off a massive return of Jews to Israel, inflamed Arab resentment and over-taxed the British colonial government. The matter was referred the newly formed United Nations that quickly recognized Israel's 1948 declaration of independence. The declaration also touched off an attack by five surrounding Arab countries.

Wars and terrorism continue to the present day, and 14 Islamic nations around the world have called for the extermination of the State of Israel.

In *The Weekly Standard* of May 11, 1998, Charles Krauthammer wrote of Israel's uniqueness: "Israel is the very embodiment of Jewish continuity: It is the only nation on earth that inhabits the same land, bears the same name, speaks the same language, and worships the same God that it did 3,000 years ago. You dig the soil and you find pottery from Davidic times, coins from Bar Kokhba, and 2,000-year-old scrolls written in a script remarkably like the one that today advertises ice cream at the corner candy store."

SACRED TEXTS

The Hebrew Bible has three parts: The Torah (Five Books of Moses), the Prophets, and the Writings, such as *Esther* and the *Psalms*. The Torah contains laws, doctrine and guidance on way of life, as well as accounts of the early history of the Jewish people and their relationship with God.

The Torah or the Pentateuch

The Hebrew Bible begins with the Pentateuch or Torah. It has also called the humash, or the Five Books of Moses. The Pentateuch covers history from the time of Abraham to the end of Jewish Exodus from Egypt and entry into the promised land of Canaan, which occurred roughly around 1200 B.C.E.

Probably edited and put in written form around the time of King David (1000 B.C.E.), the Pentateuch consists of five books (hence the name Pentateuch):

(1) *Genesis* includes the creation story of Adam and Eve, and the stories of others, such as Noah, and Joseph and his brothers.

(2) *Exodus* chronicles the liberation of the Israelites from Egypt by God through Moses, and of the years the Israelites spend wandering in the desert.

(3) *Leviticus* and *Numbers* have fewer stories than the other books and detail more laws for sacrificial offerings, the rituals of Jewish priesthood and the conduct of the people.

(4) *Deuteronomy* picks up the narrative again, repeats the Ten Commandments and several laws, and describes the final entry into the Land of Canaan and the death of Moses. Compared to other prophets in the Hebrew Bible, Moses stands alone as one who spoke to God directly and not through visions or dreams.

The Prophets

The second part of the Hebrew Bible is called Nevi'im, or Prophets. This section includes the historical books of *Joshua, Judges,* 1 and 2 *Samuel,* and 1 and 2 *Kings.* For the most part the books are named for the prophets who wrote them.

(1) Jeremiah preached that divine justice is inescapable and warned Jews against rejecting God.

(2) Isaiah believed that the covenant between Israel and God was contingent on the people's conduct. He chastised the Israelites for misbehavior that had broken the covenant, assured them of coming wrath and re-assured them that God was still merciful and would deliver them.

(3) Ezekiel warned of the destruction of Judah. His later statements foretold of a new covenant that God would make with the restored house of Israel.

The text now turns to the "Minor Prophets," who have biblical books named for them:

(1) Hosea is the last King of Israel.

(2) Amos prophesizes doom.

(3) Jonah tries to avoid his prophetic gifting only to get swallowed by a whale.

(4) Zephaniah proclaims the approach of divine judgment.

(5) Zechariah urges the Jews to rebuild the Temple of Jerusalem.

(6) Joel calls people to repent.

(7) Obadiah foretells of the destruction of the Edomites.

(8) Micah predicates the fall of Samaria and the destruction of Judah.

(9) Nahum predicates the fall of Nineveh, the capital of the Assyrian empire.

(10) Habakkuk warns of the coming Babylonian invasion.

(11) Haggai encourages exiles to return to rebuild the Temple of Jerusalem.

The Writings

The third part of the Hebrew Bible is called Ketuvim (Writings), and it includes a variety of miscellaneous books:

(1) *Psalms*, totaling 150 and making up the largest section of Ketuvim, are songs or poems of praise, thanksgiving, pleading and lamentation.

(2) *Proverbs* contains sayings attributed to Solomon and others.

(3) *Job* is about a man whom God dares Satan to tempt, undergoes tremendous suffering, and has his strong faith eventually shaken then restored. None of Job's questions about why God allows evil are answered.

(4) *Song of Songs* (also called the *Song of Solomon*) is an erotic love poem sometimes attributed as a symbolic representation of God's love for his chosen people.

(5) *Ruth* tells the story of a widow devoted to her mother-in-law, Naomi. Naomi advises Ruth about successfully remarrying, and indeed, Ruth becomes the grandmother of the King David.

(6) *Lamentations*, attributed to the prophet Jeremiah, agonizes about the imminent destruction of Jerusalem.

(7) *Ecclesiastes* is book of teachings and sometimes-cynical observations most probably authored by Solomon in his later years.

(8) *Esther* is the one book of the Bible that never mentions God but shows how a committed woman can save an entire nation from extermination.

(9) *Daniel* is a treasure of stories and end time prophesies from the Hebrew prophet in exile. Daniel's faith saves him from devouring lions and his diligence makes him an indispensable aid to a wildly erratic foreign king.

(10) *Ezra* is the autobiography and teachings of a prophet and religious reformer.

(11) *Nehemiah* recounts the work of Nehemiah, a Hebrew leader during the 5th Century.

(12) *Chronicles* I and II are books of history revolving mostly on the reign of King David.

SELECTED READINGS

BERESHIT (Book of Genesis)

Chapter 1

IN THE beginning God created the heaven and the earth. Now the earth was unformed and void, and darkness was upon the face of the deep; and the spirit of God hovered over the face of the waters. And God said: "Let there be light." And there was light.

And God saw the light, that it was good; and God divided the light from the darkness. And God called the light Day, and the darkness he called Night. And there was evening and there was morning, one day.

And God said: "Let there be a firmament in the midst of the waters, and let it divide the waters from the waters." And God made the firmament, and divided the waters which were under the firmament from the waters which were above the firmament; and it was so. And God called the firmament heaven. And there was evening and there was morning, a second day.

And God said: "Let the waters under the heaven be gathered together unto one place, and let the dry land appear." And it was so. And God called the dry land Earth, and the gathering together of the waters he called Seas; and God saw that it was good.

And God said: "Let the earth put forth grass, herb yielding seed, and fruit-tree bearing fruit after its kind, wherein is the seed thereof, upon the earth." And it was so.

And the earth brought forth grass, herb yielding seed after its kind, and tree bearing fruit, wherein is the seed thereof, after its kind; and God saw that it was good.

And there was evening and there was morning, a third day.

And God said: "Let there be lights in the firmament of the heaven to divide the day from the night; and let them be for signs, and for seasons, and for days and years; and let them be for lights in the firmament of the heaven to give light upon the earth." And it was so.

And God made the two great lights: the greater light to rule the day, and the lesser light to rule the night; and the stars. And God set them in the firmament of the heaven to give light upon the earth, and to rule over the day and over the night, and to divide the light from the darkness; and God saw that it was good.

And there was evening and there was morning, a fourth day.

And God said: "Let the waters swarm with swarms of living creatures, and let fowl fly above the earth in the open firmament of heaven." And God created the great sea-monsters, and every living creature that creepeth, wherewith the waters swarmed, after its kind, and every winged fowl after its kind; and God saw that it was good. And God blessed them, saying: 'Be fruitful, and multiply, and fill the waters in the seas, and let fowl multiply in the earth.'

And there was evening and there was morning, a fifth day.

And God said: "Let the earth bring forth the living creature after its kind, cattle, and creeping thing, and beast of the earth after its kind.' And it was so.

And God made the beast of the earth after its kind, and the cattle after their kind, and every thing that creepeth upon the ground after its kind; and God saw that it was good.

And God said: "Let us make man in our image, after our likeness; and let them have dominion over the fish of the sea, and over the fowl of the air, and over the cattle, and over all the earth, and over every creeping thing that creepeth upon the earth."

And God created man in his own image, in the image of God created he him; male and female created he them. And God blessed them; and God said unto them: "Be fruitful, and multiply, and replenish the earth, and subdue it; and have dominion over the fish of the sea, and over the fowl of the air, and over every living thing that creepeth upon the earth."

And God said: 'Behold, I have given you every herb yielding seed, which is upon the face of all the earth, and every tree, in which is the fruit of a tree yielding seed – to you it shall be for food; and to every beast of the earth, and to every fowl of the air, and to every thing that creepeth upon the earth, wherein there is a living soul, I have given every green herb for food." And it was so.

And God saw every thing that he had made, and, behold, it was very good. And there was evening and there was morning, the sixth day.

Chapter 2

And the heaven and the earth were finished, and all the host of them.

And on the seventh day God finished his work which he had made; and he rested on the seventh day from all his work which he had made. And God blessed the seventh day, and hallowed it; because that in it he rested from all his work which God in creating had made....

DEVARIM (Deuteronomy)

Chapter 6

Now this is the commandment, the statutes, and the ordinances, which the LORD your God commanded to teach you, that ye might do them in the land whither ye go over to possess it--

that thou mightest fear the LORD thy God, to keep all His statutes and His commandments, which I command thee, thou, and thy son, and thy son's son, all the days of thy life; and that thy days may be prolonged.

Hear therefore, O Israel, and observe to do it; that it may be well with thee, and that ye may increase mightily, as the LORD, the God of thy fathers, hath promised unto thee--a land flowing with milk and honey.

Hear, O Israel: the LORD our God, the LORD is one.

And thou shalt love the LORD thy God with all thy heart, and with all thy soul, and with all thy might.

And these words, which I command thee this day, shall be upon thy heart;

and thou shalt teach them diligently unto thy children, and shalt talk of them when thou sittest in thy house, and when thou walkest by the way, and when thou liest down, and when thou risest up.

And thou shalt bind them for a sign upon thy hand, and they shall be for frontlets between thine eyes.

And thou shalt write them upon the door-posts of thy house, and upon thy gates.

And it shall be, when the LORD thy God shall bring thee into the land which He swore unto thy fathers, to Abraham, to Isaac, and to Jacob, to give thee--great and goodly cities, which thou didst not build, and houses full of all good things, which thou didst not fill, and cisterns hewn out, which thou didst not hew, vineyards and olive-trees, which thou didst not plant, and thou shalt eat and be satisfied--then beware lest thou forget the LORD, who brought thee forth out of the land of Egypt, out of the house of bondage.

Thou shalt fear the LORD thy God; and Him shalt thou serve, and by His name shalt thou swear.

Ye shall not go after other gods, of the gods of the peoples that are round about you;

for a jealous God, even the LORD thy God, is in the midst of thee; lest the anger of the LORD thy God be kindled against thee, and He destroy thee from off the face of the earth.

Ye shall not try the LORD your God, as ye tried Him in Massah.

Ye shall diligently keep the commandments of the LORD your God, and His testimonies, and His statutes, which He hath commanded thee.

And thou shalt do that which is right and good in the sight of the LORD; that it may be well with thee, and that thou mayest go in and possess the good land which the LORD swore unto thy fathers,

to thrust out all thine enemies from before thee, as the LORD hath spoken.

When thy son asketh thee in time to come, saying: 'What mean the testimonies, and the statutes, and the ordinances, which the LORD our God hath commanded you?

then thou shalt say unto thy son: 'We were Pharaoh's bondmen in Egypt; and the LORD brought us out of Egypt with a mighty hand.

And the LORD showed signs and wonders, great and sore, upon Egypt, upon Pharaoh, and upon all his house, before our eyes.

And He brought us out from thence, that He might bring us in, to give us the land which He swore unto our fathers.

And the LORD commanded us to do all these statutes, to fear the LORD our God, for our good always, that He might preserve us alive, as it is at this day.

And it shall be righteousness unto us, if we observe to do all this commandment before the LORD our God, as He hath commanded us.'

CORE BELIEFS

God was not created by something else. God transcends time and history.

Life begins with the one identified in Hebrew as Elohim. A plural noun, Elohim is understood to have a singular referent, the one true and sovereign God. This is seen clearly in the fact that the verb created is singular in Hebrew: one God and only one God created everything, both spiritual and material. The Hebrew monotheistic view diverged starkly from the entire ancient world in which polytheism was the norm.

After establishing that he is Elohim, God revealed his name to Moses as Yahweh, which is a form of the verb "to be." It is made up of four Hebrew letters is YHWH and is unpronounceable. Some scholars translate the name as Yahweh although no ancient Jew would use that word. The word was so sacred that early scribes, before writing an indication of it, had to cleanse themselves ritually.

The Hebrew Bible has some names for God that could be pronounced, such as Adoni, which means my Lord, and El Shaddai. Jewish mystics called God *Hamakom*, the place of the endless one.

Judaism teaches that God is the source of everything, including all goodness and all evil, but he has given people free will. God offers the choice of life and goodness over death and sin, but he does not compel one to choose. God revealed the Torah, a code of law and spiritually enlightening stories, which people should follow to show love and obedience to God.

Judaism believes that God chose the Jewish people as vessels of his covenant and as witnesses of his love. Being chosen as part of his covenant does not make the Jewish people better than other peoples. The covenant relationship with God makes Jews only a carrier of God's words and will.

Judaism has a long tradition of arguing with God. In the Hebrew Bible, Abraham contends with God to save the cities of Sodom and Gomorrah. The questioning of God is not a sin; such questioning is encouraged as a way of coming to understand the sacred texts and the ways of God in the world.

God demands justice in this world. In daily lives and businesses, he commands honesty and integrity. God's revelation of the Ten Commandments in the Hebrew Bible is the cornerstone of Western morality and jurisprudence.

Jews believe that God is the creator of the world and, because of this, he owns everything. He will one day send a Messiah to redeem the world from evil and usher in an age of peace and tranquility and then resurrect the dead and bring them back to life. Because he is the God of

all people, he grants the blessings of heaven to the righteous of all peoples.

BRANCHES OF JUDAISM

Modern Judaism is divided into four movements—Orthodox, Conservative, Reform and Reconstructionist.

Orthodox

Orthodox Jews are the most traditionally observant Jews. Men al-
ways wear a head covering when going out, and women dress modestly.
Men and women are separated during prayer services. All Orthodox
Jews keep *kosher* (follow strict dietary laws) all the time, both at home and
out of the home. No women can be rabbis or cantors. No Orthodox
Jews will allow their children to marry unconverted non-Jews. Orthodox
Judaism has two main divisions:

> (1) Hasidic Judaism. Hasidic Jews do not generally send their chil-
> dren to any secular schools or universities. At parties men and
> women sit and dance separately. Hasidic Jews follow the teaching of
> a *rebbe*, a mystical wonder-working rabbi who is descended from a
> line of other Hasidic rebbes.

> (2) Modern Orthodox Judaism. Unlike the Hasidic rebbe, a Modern
> Orthodox rabbi need not be the heir to a rabbinic dynasty. Men and
> women are separated in prayer but not always at parties. Modern
> Orthodox Jews send their children to secular universities after they
> have had their worldview set in Jewish parochial schools.

Conservative

Conservative Jews follow a less strict interpretation of Jewish law
than Orthodox Jews does. All Conservative Jewish men wear head coverings in prayer, and many wear them all the time. Men and women are
not separated in prayer. Most Conservative Jews keep kosher at home,

but some will eat in non-kosher restaurants. Conservative Judaism opposes inter-marriage to non-Jews. Conservative Jews sometimes send their children to parochial schools. Women can become Conservative rabbis and cantors.

Reform

The Reform movement in Judaism represents a more liberal interpretation of Jewish law than Conservative Judaism. Some reform Jews and rabbis wear head coverings in prayer, but very few wear them all the time. Very few Reform Jews keep kosher at home or outside the home.

Women can be rabbis and cantors in the Reform Movement. Reform Jews will rarely send their children to Jewish parochial schools.

Reconstructionist

Reconstructionist Jews are similar to Reform Jews, but they practice Jewish traditional historical customs like keeping kosher. Rabbi Mordecai Kaplan was the founder of Reconstructionist Judaism, and he focused more on the Jewish traditions than on God as the commander of and reveler of Jewish law.

JUDAISM IN THE MARKETPLACE

Jewish ethics are summed up in the Ten Commandments and in the philosophy of "an eye for an eye and a tooth for a tooth." The latter sounds harsh today, but it was an enormous advance on the take-no-prisoners ethics of the societies that surrounded the Jewish people in the days of Moses. The non-Jewish principle of the time was a life for an eye, and if I cannot kill you, I will get a member of your family. This was the whole basis of feuding, which was widespread even in the West until recent history.

The Jewish Golden Rule is contained in *Leviticus* 19:18: "Thou shall love thy neighbor as thyself."

In the Hebrew Bible Job serves as a prime example of patience as a virtue. Job was an innocent man who refused to curse God despite his sufferings. The rabbinic teachings about patience are reflected by a famous passage from *Avot* 2:16 of the Talmud: "You are not required to finish the work, but you are also not free to refrain from doing the work."

Proverbs 22 states, "A good name is to be more desired than great riches." In the same chapter, one aspect of a good name is given as, "Work hard and stick to it, do not let laziness or sleep rob you of success." *Proverbs* 12:11 reiterates, "He who works his land will have abundant food, but he who chases fantasies lacks judgment." *Proverbs* 12:27 emphasizes, "A slothful man does not roast his prey, but the precious possession of a man is diligence."

According to Jewish law, if you deceive someone, you are also guilty of violating the commandment against stealing because you are stealing knowledge.

The Hebrew Bible insists that one maintains honest weights and measures in business. The rabbinic tradition continues the demand for honesty. According to the Talmud, *Shabbat* 31a, when a person appears before the throne of judgment, the first question asked is not, "Have you believed in God?" or, "Have you prayed or performed your ritual acts?" but rather, "Have you dealt honorably, faithfully in all your dealings with your fellowmen?"

Rabbi Yisrael Lipkin, better known as Rav Yisrael Salanter, the founder of the 19th Century Mussar movement in Eastern Europe, taught that just as one checks carefully to make sure food is kosher, so too should one check to see if money is earned in a kosher fashion.

But here we go again! While the teaching about honesty in business dealings leaves little room for misconduct in the marketplace, not all Jews adhere to their faith equally. Moreover, religious law does not cover everything, and some Jews have found a number of loopholes. Practitioners of Judaism who are dishonest in business dealings can offer justification (to their own consciences at any rate) as to why they did not keep to the spirit of Jewish law.

REFERENCES AND FURTHER READING

Dorff, Elliot N. *Contemporary Jewish Ethics and Morality: A Reader.* New York: Oxford University Press USA, 1995.

Pava, Moses L. *Business Ethics: A Jewish Perspective (Library of Jewish Law and Ethics).* Jersey City: Ktav Publishing House, 1997.

Rosenthal, Donna. *The Israelis: Ordinary People in an Extraordinary Land.* New York: Free Press, 2003.

Tamari, Meir. *The Challenge of Wealth: A Jewish Perspective on Earning and Spending Money.* Lanham: Jason Aronson, 1995.

_____. *Al Chet: Sins in the Marketplace.* Latham: Rowman & Littlefield Publishers, 1996.

_____. *With All Your Possessions: Jewish Ethics and Economic Life.* Lanham: Jason Aronson, 1999.

Wagschal, Rabbi S. *Torah Guide for the Businessman.* Nanuet: Feldheim Publishers, 1990.

PART FIVE

⊙

THE RELIGION OF SECULAR POST-MODERNISM

CHAPTER 10

SECULAR POSTMODERNISM

Do no harm to the earth, she is your mother.

Being is more important than having.

Never promote yourself at another's expense.

Hold life sacred; treat it with reverence.

Allow each person the dignity of his or her labor.

Open your home to the wayfarer.

Arthur Dobrin, *A Humanist Code of Ethics*

Secular Postmodernism does not recognize any god-like beings or metaphysical forces. There is the natural world only—no divine power, no God, no angels—because there isn't scientific evidence for anything but the natural world. Human pronouncements on the supernatural are so much hot air that vainly tries to verify what can't be substantiated.

What is man without God? A remarkable animal. He was originally nothing more than a bottom feeder in the primordial ooze, but through genetic mutation, random chance and multi-millions of years, he became something more biologically complex. Like every other animal from aardvarks to zebras, he needs food to survive. If he is fit, he will hunt successfully and fill his stomach. If not, he'll die.

He is a social animal on one hand. On the other, he has appetites for sex and territory that make him a warring animal.

Unlike other animals, he can imagine suffering, not merely remember pain. He can look to the future. He can plan for it but usually not very well.

Or perhaps he is just a consumer of goods and services. Economics, specifically the clash between labor and capital, is the sole determinate of human history.

Or if you like, where we are now as a species was determined by gender or race, psychology or prejudice, maybe many combinations of what we can't or won't control.

No matter what you think, the sun will go out in four billion years, and it won't make any difference how we get however far we go because this physical world will all be gone.

Can one act morally within the context of existential bleakness? Certainly. You can do what feels good. You can do what your parents taught you. On your own you can figure out that certain activities don't endear you to the neighbors, and who wants problems with them? Individually, you can be selfless, honest and hard working in spite of everyone around you telling you to look out for only yourself. Globally, you can advocate for peace, the disclosure of UFO files, the recycling of beer cans.

One person may say that she is humanist, a moral relativist and a strict materialist. Another may describe himself as a hedonist, a stoic, a cynic and an environmentalist. These all have manifestation in what is broadly called Secular Postmodernism. Individually and lumped together they are philosophies, not religions.

There is some common ground between philosophy and religion. Many philosophies take up the questions of what is good and how people should act. In providing guidelines on living, philosophies have ethics, just as religions do. But religions differ from philosophies in several ways.

(1) Only a religion has rituals. Yes, people can follow rituals without believing in their import, but we are talking about religious people who do believe. From that perspective, only a religion has holy days. Only a religion has ceremonies to sanctify birth, marriage and death. Rituals are the clearest way of differentiating religions from philosophies.

Some religions, such as Buddhism and Confucianism, have often been termed philosophies by Westerners because outsiders have looked for a transcendent God and did not find one. Zen Buddhists do not teach about a Supreme Being because first and foremost the goal for adherents is to find enlightenment within themselves. Other Buddhist sects, such as Pure Land, do believe in a transcendent God. However, because of their rituals, ceremonies and venerated texts, Buddhism and Confucianism have more in common with religions than with pure philosophies like Marxism.

(2) Philosophies use reason to figure out what is true, and religions use both reason and revelation.

On one hand, reason depends solely upon the use of unaided human thinking. Reason does not appeal to the authority of God or to tradition to establish truth. On the other hand, religion often depends on revelation, a gift of knowledge given in a holy text or directly from God to a prophet. To accept reason you have to think, but to accept revelation you have to add belief.

(3) Religions teach that miracles, which appear to supersede commonly held beliefs about nature, are actually real. Miraculous events are not metaphorical or symbolic tales that represent some divine principle. In nature, bushes do not burn without being consumed, and people do not rise from the dead.

Miracles are examples of God's power and love for people of faith. They are also classic examples of how religions can seem irrational to philosophers who seek to prove all truth by reason.

Religions and philosophies are like two circles that intersect. The part they share is the search for what is true about life here on earth. The belief that stealing and murder are wrong is a place where the circles overlap. The beliefs in Moses' splitting the Red Sea or in Buddha's turning rain into a shower of flowers are parts of the religious circle that cannot touch the circle of secular philosophy.

HISTORY

In every culture in every era there have always been individuals who do not have faith and cannot believe in God. The history that follows tries to show how masses of people have reached the same point.

The Enlightenment is generally placed between 1680 and 1860 C.E. The period started with the scientific revolution of the 17th Century, reaching its epitome with Sir Isaac Newton. As time progressed, the industrial and agricultural revolutions changed the face of town and country. But if William Blake's "dark Satanic mills" blighted the landscape, there also was great romantic hope that technological advancement would bring about humanity's ability to control the environment to the good of both man and nature. Thereby God would be pleased with a world in harmony.

Modernism extended from the writings of Charles Darwin in the mid-19th Century and petered out by the end of the 20th as scientists and social commentators excised God (and all religions) from any hope of helping harmony. The worldview of Modernism, and the philosophies that orbited its worldview, became increasingly materialist. By the end of the 19th Century, the avant-garde in French architecture were describing a house as "a machine" that contained people.

Some place the beginning of Postmodernism with the Nazi terror and the U.S. atomic bombings of Japan. More look to the 1970s as a starting point. Postmodernism embraces all the materialism preceding, but only with cynicism and subjectivity. Adding Secular to Postmodernism emphasizes that God need not apply. Secular Postmodernism can contain some elements of Eastern mysticism but mostly as a way to get back at the prejudices of Western religions and rationalism. What distinguishes Postmodernism from Modernism is a bleak sense of absurdity. Progress is haphazard: witness World War II and the coming Ice Age to be brought on by humanity's disregard for Mother Earth. You can't count on anything. Everything is relative.

Although a pure Secular Postmodernist would not think that history can be informative of anything but the author's own biases, it is necessary to look back at how ancient Greek philosophers spoke of the gods worshipped by common folk. The likes of Socrates and Aristotle regarded those gods as useful but phantasmagorical symbols. From time to time during the history of western civilization, to hold similar views was either fashionable or very dangerous.

For almost two centuries, from the mid-16th until the mid-17th Centuries C.E., an Englishman who had strong religious beliefs—to purify the state sanctioned church, to separate from it, to pray or plot for the return of Catholicism, to shrug it all off— was prudent to keep those thoughts to himself.

Similar and sometimes bloodier consequences for speaking out took place throughout Europe. A reaction in the 17th Century was the coinage of the term Enlightenment. On the backside of the Enlightenment, Christianity's Dark Ages smothered the supposed pagan glory of Imperial Rome. Then the light of the Renaissance was snuffed out by religious conflicts. But presto! The Enlightenment birthed scientific advancement, the Industrial Revolution and true religious understanding in the form of Higher Criticism.

Higher Criticism started with theologians in Germany, and blitz-krieged across Europe and into the New World. The basic assumption was that the Bible needed to be studied as text only, setting aside any claims of divine inspiration and pigeon-holing the miracles as folklore. The conclusions were virtually inevitable. In spite of the fact that key conclusions did not fare well under coming discoveries in archeology and in linguistics, Higher Criticism by other names has strong influence on universities and seminaries today.

To get to Secular Postmodernism, religion needed to be incrementally killed, but in the process revivals would break out. The First Great Awakening spread from the American Colonies to the British Isles. Philosophically, it led to American calls for autonomy and ultimately to the Revolutionary War. The Second Great Awakening of an independent America gave new fire to the abolitionist movement and once again forced the issue of war, this time between the Northern states and the slave-holding Southern.

During the widespread religious revivals in America of the 18th and 19th Centuries, there were outspoken "free thinkers," otherwise known as atheists. Nearly every settlement had a free thinker who was usually regarded as an eccentric but loveable fool. A sea change in respectability (and the influence that goes with it) followed in the wake of Darwinism.

In the baldest terms, Darwinists introduced monkeys as the real parents of humanity, not Adam and Eve created in the *Imago Dei*, the Latin phrase meaning "the image of God." Preparation for the acceptance of that notion came not so much from scientists like Darwin as from philosophers.

Radically new ideas abounded—the "turn to the subject" of Descartes, Immanuel Kant's insistence that the "autonomous self" is the only valid guide for moral action, and the social contract theories of Hobbes, Rousseau and Locke. In the late 1800s, a name was given for it all—Philosophical Pragmatism.

With materialism at its heart, Philosophical Pragmatism attempted to develop a comprehensive philosophy of life that could satisfy the need of most people to make sense of existence. Therein was the root of Modernism from which would blossom Secular Postmodernism.

Pragmatists enthusiastically embraced Darwinism and recognized that an entire new worldview could be built from its fundamental principles. The 20th Century saw Darwinian and Pragmatic bases for modern anthropological and psychological theorists. Traditional theologians retreated from academia while radically liberal and militantly conservative activists promoted political agendas with religious zeal.

Dostoevsky said that if God is dead, everything is justifiable. In humanity's search for morality and happiness outside of God, all three have been lost—God, morality and happiness.

SACRED TEXTS

No writings are sacred to Secular Postmodernists because there is no absolute truth. They favor and give great authority, however, to Western nonreligious literature that draws from great minds of philosophy, such as Plato, Socrates and Spinoza, and from major contributors in science, such as Einstein, Darwin, and Huxley. Additionally, Secular Postmodernists tend to value Eastern mystical and "New Age" literature, such as the works of Deepak Chopra, Eckhart Tolle and Barbara Marx Hubbard, as well as the writings of prime movers in Enlightenment Era politics, such as Voltaire, Mary Wollstonecraft, and the Thomases, Jefferson and Paine.

SELECTED READINGS

From the pamphlet *THE RELIGION OF DEISM COMPARED TO THE CHRISTIAN RELIGION*

by Thomas Paine

Every person, of whatever religious denomination he may be, is a DEIST in the first article of his Creed. Deism, from the Latin word Deus, God, is the belief of a God, and this belief is the first article of every man's creed.

It is on this article, universally consented to by all humankind that the Deist builds his church, and here he rests. Whenever we step aside from this article, by mixing it with articles of human invention, we wander into a labyrinth of uncertainty and fable, and become exposed to every kind of imposition by pretenders to revelation.

The Persian shows the Zend-Avesta of Zoroaster, the lawgiver of Persia, and calls it the divine law; the Bramin shows the Shaster, revealed, he says, by God to Brama, and given to him out of a cloud; the Jew shows what he calls the law of Moses, given, he says, by God, on the Mount Sinai; the Christian shows a collection of books and epistles, written by nobody knows who, and called the New Testament; and the Mahometan shows the Koran, given, he says, by God to Mahomet: each of these calls itself revealed religion, and the only true Word of God, and this the followers of each profess to believe from the habit of education, and each believes the others are imposed upon.

But when the divine gift of reason begins to expand itself in the mind and calls man to reflection, he then reads and contemplates God and His works, and not in the books pretending to be revelation. The creation is the Bible of the true believer in God. Everything in this vast volume inspires him with sublime ideas of the Creator. The little and paltry, and often obscene, tales of the Bible sink into wretchedness when put in comparison with this mighty work.

From The Humanist Manifesto
Written in 1933 by Raymond Bragg and published with thirty-four signatories including Anton J. Carlson, John Dewey, John H. Dietrich, R. Lester Mondale, Charles Francis Potter, Curtis W. Reese, and Edwin H. Wilson

The time has come for widespread recognition of the radical changes in religious beliefs throughout the modern world. The time is past for mere revision of traditional attitudes. Science and economic change have disrupted the old beliefs. Religions the world over are under the necessity of coming to terms with new conditions created by a vastly increased knowledge and experience. In every field of human activity, the vital movement is now in the direction of a candid and explicit humanism. In order that religious humanism may be better understood we, the undersigned, desire to make certain affirmations which we believe the facts of our contemporary life demonstrate.

There is great danger of a final, and we believe fatal, identification of the word religion with doctrines and methods which have lost their significance and which are powerless to solve the problem of human living in the 20th Century. Religions have always been means for realizing the highest values of life. Their end has been accomplished through the interpretation of the total environing situation (theology or world view), the sense of values resulting there from (goal or ideal), and the technique (cult), established for realizing the satisfactory life. A change in any of these factors results in alteration of the outward forms of religion. This fact explains the changefulness of religions through the centuries. But through all changes religion itself remains constant in its quest for abiding values, an inseparable feature of human life.

Today man's larger understanding of the universe, his scientific achievements, and deeper appreciation of brotherhood, have created a situation which requires a new statement of the means and purposes of religion. Such a vital, fearless, and frank religion capable of furnishing adequate social goals and personal satisfactions may appear to many people as a complete break with the past. While this age does owe a vast debt to the traditional religions, it is nonetheless obvious that any religion that can hope to be a synthesizing and dynamic force for today must be shaped for the needs of this age. To establish such a religion is a major necessity of the present. It is a responsibility which rests upon this generation. We therefore affirm the following:

FIRST: Religious humanists regard the universe as self-existing and not created.

SECOND: Humanism believes that man is a part of nature and that he has emerged as a result of a continuous process.

THIRD: Holding an organic view of life, humanists find that the traditional dualism of mind and body must be rejected.

FOURTH: Humanism recognizes that man's religious culture and civilization, as clearly depicted by anthropology and history, are the product of a gradual development due to his interaction with his natural environment and with his social heritage. The individual born into a particular culture is largely molded by that culture.

FIFTH: Humanism asserts that the nature of the universe depicted by modern science makes unacceptable any supernatural or cosmic guarantees of human values. Obviously humanism does not deny the possibility of realities as yet undiscovered, but it does insist that the way to determine the existence and value of any and all realities is by means of intelligent inquiry and by the assessment of their relations to human needs. Religion must formulate its hopes and plans in the light of the scientific spirit and method.

SIXTH: We are convinced that the time has passed for theism, deism, modernism, and the several varieties of "new thought".

SEVENTH: Religion consists of those actions, purposes, and experiences which are humanly significant. Nothing human is alien to the religious. It includes labor, art, science, philosophy, love, friendship, recreation—all that is in its degree expressive of intelligently satisfying human living. The distinction between the sacred and the secular can no longer be maintained.

EIGHTH: Religious Humanism considers the complete realization of human personality to be the end of man's life and seeks its development and fulfillment in the here and now. This is the explanation of the humanist's social passion.

NINTH: In the place of the old attitudes involved in worship and prayer the humanist finds his religious emotions expressed in a heightened sense of personal life and in a cooperative effort to promote social well being.

TENTH: It follows that there will be no uniquely religious emotions and attitudes of the kind hitherto associated with belief in the supernatural.

ELEVENTH: Man will learn to face the crises of life in terms of his knowledge of their naturalness and probability. Reasonable and manly attitudes will be fostered by education and supported by custom. We assume that humanism will take the path of social and mental hygiene and discourage sentimental and unreal hopes and wishful thinking.

TWELFTH: Believing that religion must work increasingly for joy in living, religious humanists aim to foster the creative in man and to encourage achievements that add to the satisfactions of life.

THIRTEENTH: Religious humanism maintains that all associations and institutions exist for the fulfillment of human life. The intelligent evaluation, transformation, control and direction of such associations and institutions with a view to the enhancement of human life is the purpose and program of humanism. Certainly religious institutions, their ritualistic forms, ecclesiastical methods, and communal activities must be reconstituted as rapidly as experience allows, in order to function effectively in the modern world.

FOURTEENTH: The humanists are firmly convinced that existing acquisitive and profit-motivated society has shown itself to be inadequate and that a radical change in methods, controls, and motives must be instituted. A socialized and cooperative economic order must be established to the end that the equitable distribution of the means of life be possible. The goal of humanism is a free and universal society in which people voluntarily and intelligently cooperate for the common good. Humanists demand a shared life in a shared world.

FIFTEENTH AND LAST: We assert that humanism will: (a) affirm life rather than deny it; (b) seek to elicit the possibilities of life, not flee from them; and (c) endeavor to establish the conditions of a satisfactory life for all, not merely for the few. By this positive morale and intention humanism will be guided, and from this perspective and alignment the techniques and efforts of humanism will flow.

CORE BELIEFS

Secular Postmodernism rejects Modernism's autonomous individualism and all that follows from it. Rather than seeing humanity as an ocean of individuals, Secular Postmodernists think of humans as "social constructs."

Rather than conceiving of the mind as a mirror of nature, Secular Postmodernists argue that we view reality through the lens of culture. Our socio-economic backgrounds, our upbringings, our friends, our educational levels and everything else about us influence the way we perceive every situation. Even when we simply observe a situation, we interact with it and change it to some degree.

In the place of objective truth and comprehensive worldviews, Secular Postmodernists honor "local narratives" or stories about reality that "work" for particular communities. Beyond that community they have no validity. Indeed, Secular Postmodernists reject the language of truth and reality in favor of literary terms like narrative and story. It is all about interpretation.

Secular Postmodernists argue that the pretense of objective truth always does violence because it excludes minority voices, invalidates contrary worldviews and marginalizes the vulnerable by scripting them out of the story. Claims of truth, we are told, are essentially tools to legitimatize those in power.

Because of these attitudes about subjectivity and truth, Secular Postmodernists believes that everything must be questioned. Questioning helps us to understand more fully what affects the way we think. Only by recognizing our inherent and inescapable subjectivity can we see more clearly.

The result: postmodernism is all about self-awareness.

BRANCHES OF SECULAR POSTMODERNISM

Secular Postmodernism is a large umbrella covering many different views. Among the biggest schools of thought within Secular Postmodernism are:

Atheistic

Atheists reject any belief in God or gods.

Scientist/Naturalistic

Scientists/Naturalists believe the world can be understood in scientific terms without any spiritual or supernatural explanations.

New Age Movement

The New Age Movement is free flowing and broad in Western culture. It is characterized by an individualistic, eclectic approach to spiritual exploration. It has some attributes of an emerging religion but is currently a loose network of spiritual seekers, gurus and psychic healers.

SECULAR POSTMODERNISM IN THE MARKETPLACE

Secular Postmodernism's approach to business ethics is that there are none. To suggest an absolute truth is absolutely intolerable. It is arrogant for anyone to assert they grasp anything more than personal history.

The concept of not having a religion is relatively new to the world. The vast majority of people throughout history have had a commitment to some sort of absolute, such God, or the gods, or an impersonal principle that they believed guided the world and life.

Secular Post-modernists are optimistic because they can make up their own meanings for the purposes of being in business. Most ascribe to ethics that can be loosely termed positive and humane. But they are simultaneously pessimistic because there is no meaning or purpose in life to believe in.

Some Secular Postmodernists are highly "moral," meaning that they are committed to certain principles, even if those principles are immoral from a traditional point of view. Others are moral as long as it is convenient. Still others are concerned only about not being caught.

The key point for a Secular Postmodernist is that you cannot fault any of them for anything. Each has constructed his or her own meaning, purpose or philosophy when it comes to commerce. You never know if the ethical standards practiced last week will be the standards that operate next week. The Secular Postmodernist does not know either. If "reality" changes, so do business ethics.

REFERENCES AND FURTHER READING

Adkins, Gary Y. *Diversity Beyond the Numbers: Business Vitality, Ethics & Identity in the 21st Century.* Long Beach: GDI Press, 2003.

Crane, Andrew. *Business Ethics: A European Perspective: Managing Corporate Citizenship and Sustainability in the Age of Globalization.* New York: Oxford University Press USA, 2004.

Ferrell, O.C. *Business Ethics: Ethical Decision Making and Cases.* Boston: Houghton Mifflin Company, 2004.

Grayling, A.C. *Meditations for the Humanist: Ethics for a Secular Age.* New York: Oxford University Press USA, 2002.

Solomon, Robert C. *A Better Way to Think About Business: How Personal Integrity Leads to Corporate Success.* New York: Oxford University Press USA, 2003.

Solomon, Robert C. *Ethics and Excellence: Cooperation and Integrity in Business (The Ruffin Series in Business Ethics).* New York: Oxford University Press USA, 1993.

Witzel, Morgen. *The Emergence of Business Ethics.* London: Thoemmes Continuum, 2002.

PART SIX

◉

EPILOGUE

CHAPTER 11

AFTERWORD

When morality comes up against profit,
it is seldom that profit loses.

Congresswomen Shirley Chisholm

There are over 6 billion people on this planet trying to figure out how to live life. Of these 6 billion, over 5 billion have some religious faith. 2.1 billion are Christian; 1.3 billion are Muslim; 1.1 billion are Secular Postmodernists; 900 million are Hindu; 394 million are Confucians; 376 million are Buddhist; 23 million are Sikh; 14 million follow Judaism; and 4 million are Shintoists.

All of these religions have a great deal to say about business ethics and have extensive literature and legal codes on how one should treat others in business and in life.

For example, all of the religions we discussed in this book teach an equivalent of The Golden Rule and have strong ethical stances on honesty. If people of faith applied their religion's teachings on either one of these principals, virtually all unethical behavior in business would be eliminated overnight.

In *A Word to the Reader* at the beginning of this book, I shared how a business I owned had strategic relationships with two companies that were very religious in their organizational culture. Therefore I was surprised by how dishonest and unethical those companies were in their business dealings. The religious culture in both cases happened to be Christian. One business was Roman Catholic; the other, Southern Baptist.

Christianity clearly teaches ethical behavior in business, and as mentioned earlier in these pages, is the *de facto* standard for international commerce. Why then was I so unlucky as to have to deal with two examples of blatant hypocrisy?

On a macro level businesses usually define themselves by the goods or services they provide. Seldom do corporations define their cultures in religious terms. You don't drive a Shinto or a Christian car. You drive a Toyota or a Ford.

On a micro level executives and employees may do their tasks within a personal context of religious belief. As we have seen with all religions, it is possible to have faith and not be ethical. Most people do not think deeply about their faith or its application to everyday life. As a practical mater, then, personal faith is influenced more by the surrounding worldly culture than what is taught by the priest or the mullah. Perhaps the businesspersons who feel the greatest need to label themselves "devout" are the very people most unconsciously influenced by sleazy television soap operas.

The Rule of Three

For what it worth, I categorized religious people in business under three broad categories.

(1) They do not see that their values have anything to do with their business practices. They simply follow good professional ethics without considering religious origins. They want to be part of an honest business that makes a decent profit and can pay out living wages.

(2) They are consciously or unconsciously greedy and will do whatever needed to make a lot of money.

(3) They wrestle with questions. Is this the right way to make money? Am I making too much money? Am I treating my clients and my suppliers fairly? Am I making too little money for my stakeholders? What is the impact of my business on my community and the environment?

In my case, the people with whom I dealt fell into the second category. They were greedy.

There is something in the human heart that recognizes what is right regardless of the system of belief one embraces. Some people apply concepts of right and wrong in their business dealings. Others do not.

Broadly, there is fundamental conflict between two ethical systems that have nothing to do with specific religions. One is based on notions of fairness, justice and humanity (which most people accept in theory). The other stands on contrary values of greed, power and self-gratification. It is important to be clear about this fundamental conflict when doing business at all.

INDEX

About the Author

Writer and speaker Todd Albertson is an expert on organizational behavior, global business practices and religious worldviews. His commonsense take on these issues derives from both his academic training and from his real world business experiences.

Todd graduated in 1988 with a BA degree with a special focus on International Business. He earned an MBA in 1995. In 2005 he graduated with a PhD in Theology & Culture.

Todd worked for a venture capital firm, was an evangelist for the worldwide leader in computer software and solutions, was CEO of a transportation and logistics company, and founded a new media dot com.

More information about Todd can be found on his website at www.toddalbertson.com.

Printed in the United States
101148LV00003B/97/A